The Power of the Powerless

Jürgen Moltmann

The Power of the
Powerless

HARPER & ROW, PUBLISHERS, San Francisco
Cambridge, Hagerstown, New York, Philadelphia
London, Mexico City, São Paulo, Sydney

Translated by Margaret Kohl from the German *Ohne Macht mächtig*, first published 1981 by Christian Kaiser Verlag, Munich, with additional material supplied by the author. (The present chapter 17 first appeared in *Diakonie* 8.2, March/April 1982, 120—30; chapter 18 is previously unpublished.) © Jürgen Moltmann 1981, 1982.

FIRST U.S. EDITION

Library of Congress Cataloging in Publication Data

Moltmann, Jürgen.
THE POWER OF THE POWERLESS.

Translation of: Ohne Macht mächtig.
1. Lutheran Church—Sermons.   2. Sermons, English—
Translations from German.   3. Sermons, German—Translations into English.   I. Title.
BX8066.M603613   1983   252'.041   82-48403
ISBN 0-06-065907-6

83   84   85   86   87   10   9   8   7   6   5   4   3   2   1

*To my friends in Korea
in a common hope*

Contents

Preface

The aim of a sermon is not merely to make a statement. Sermons are also meant to communicate something that has been experienced. What they seek to state is found in the biblical testimonies which relate the history of powerless men and women with the God who makes them live. What they intend to convey is experienced in the presence of the divine Spirit, who calls the unworthy, opens people who are closed in on themselves, disarms the aggressive and encourages the powerless to hope.

Sermons mediate between the text of the biblical testimonies, and poor and helpless people today. It is out of this mediation that the community of Christ comes into being. People gather together to listen to the words of the Bible, translated into the language of the present; and they disperse again in order to bring the energies of the divine Spirit which they have experienced to the people with whom they share their day-to-day lives. The community of God exists in this gathering and in this dispersion. And the sermon participates in the same double movement, drawing its listeners and sending them out. This means that the preacher has to remember, not merely the attraction of his text, but also the mission of the Spirit in the act required at this particular moment of the present. The sermon stands between text and act. So anyone who preaches must remember the consequences his text has for the acts and for the suffering of the congregation to whom – among whom – he is speaking.

Experiences of powerlessness are now the order of the day. They are the experiences we face in every sector of life. Everywhere we come up against limits which we never envisaged. There are limits to economic growth; limits to the readiness for political action; limits to personal self-realization. It is not these limits themselves that are the problem. The problem is the way in which we meet the experience of limitation. Our reactions can be fatal. If we react with anger, we run our heads against a wall. If we react with resignation, we destroy ourselves. But living means experiencing impotence without giving up. It means accepting limits without becoming resigned. Yet where can we find the strength that is made perfect in weakness?

All the biblical testimonies speak to us about the power of the powerless. This was the way in which the people of Israel in their poverty experienced God. This was the way in which the crucified Christ experienced God. And this too is the experience of the divine Spirit today: God's Spirit is the power of the powerless, in us as well. Let us discover him in us and us in him. The power of the powerless – that is the name of God, the true God.

These sermons, taken from those I have preached over the last ten years, have brought me to ask increasingly about the vital energy that has sustained oppressed, imprisoned and saddened men and women in their weakness. They have made me look more and more earnestly for the assurance that lays hold of people as they tread the path of Christian discipleship. It is not least my friends in Korea who have drawn my thoughts in this direction, and it is to them that this book is therefore dedicated.

The sermons are arranged according to their biblical texts, not chronologically, because it is the texts that are the important thing. I have only occasionally added prayers, because prayers normally spring out of a specific situation and cannot be repeated.

Finally, sermons belong within the congregation – the community of Christians who meet together in the Lord's Supper, baptize, and share a common life. The final two lectures are intended to bring out this point. Most of the sermons were preached in university services in the Stiftskirche in Tübingen.

Tübingen, Pentecost 1981   Jürgen Moltmann

1 Surviving with Noah

And God blessed Noah and his sons, and said to them,
'Be fruitful and multiply, and fill the earth.
The fear of you and the dread of you
shall be upon every beast of the earth,
and upon every bird of the air,
upon everything that creeps on the ground
and all the fish of the sea;
into your hand they are delivered.
Every moving thing that lives shall be food for you;
and as I gave you the green plants, I give you everything.
Only you shall not eat flesh with its life,
that is, its blood.
For your lifeblood I will surely require a reckoning;
of every beast I will require it,
and of man I will require the life of man,
for he is your brother.
Whoever sheds the blood of man,
by man shall his blood be shed;
for God made man in his own image.
And you, be fruitful and multiply,
bring forth abundantly on the earth and (rule) over it.
I set my bow in the cloud,
and it shall be a sign of the covenant between me and the earth.
When I bring clouds over the earth
and the bow is seen in the clouds,
I will remember my covenant
which is between me and you and every living creature of all
    flesh;
and the waters shall never again become a flood

to destroy all flesh.
When the bow is in the clouds,
I will look upon it and remember the everlasting covenant
between God and every living creature of all flesh
that is upon the earth!'
And God said to Noah,
'This is the sign of the covenant which I have established
between me and all flesh that is upon the earth'
                                        (Genesis 9.1–7; 13–17).

The text I have chosen can be found in the Book of Genesis. It tells us
of the blessing given to Noah, and the covenant God made with him
after the Flood. To help us to understand the message of this passage,
let us first of all try to imagine the situation in which these promises
of God are uttered.

The story of the Flood begins in prehistoric times. Genesis 6 tells
us how it came about:

> And God saw the earth, and behold, it was corrupt; for all flesh
> had corrupted their way upon the earth. And God said to Noah,
> 'I have determined to make an end of all flesh; for the earth is filled
> with violence through them; behold, I will destroy them with the
> earth' (6.12f.).

Then the great flood comes out of Chaos and destroys all life on
earth. Only Noah and the beasts in his ark survive. With them God
makes a new covenant and to them he gives his blessing.

But is this really a story belonging to primaeval times? Is it not
rather a reminder of the future? The earth is full of violence:

- In the year 2000 most of the raw materials the industrial
  countries use in their economies today will be exhausted.
- In 2000 the air and the water will be so polluted that they can
  no longer be cleansed.
- In 2000 hundreds of animal species and thousands of plants we
  know today will have become extinct.
- At the moment people are spending more than a billion dollars
  every day on armaments, to threaten one another and to protect

themselves against one another. How much is intimidation and defence going to cost in the year 2000?

- In 2000 there will be 2,500 cities of mass poverty and misery like the Calcutta we know today.
- The neuroses of fear and aggression are spreading like epidemics. How sick is humanity going to be in 2000?
- Will there be a year 2000 at all?

The breakdown in the balance of nature and in many of the social systems that we know is not merely something to be feared; it is something we can actually foresee. And this time we shall not need a natural catastrophe like the Flood to bring down the divine judgment on human beings. All that is needed to exterminate human beings and all other living things on earth is human wickedness, just by itself. We no longer have to wait for a divine punishment. We are already experiencing it. We are already living and dying now, today, in the very midst of God's judgment on the wickedness on earth. We ourselves are the guilty ones. We ourselves are the judges. For God, as Paul already grasped, has given people up 'to their base minds'. The divine wrath from heaven manifests itself in human godforsakenness. This is our 'Flood': the fact that we have been 'given up' to our own wickedness. The end of the world is in our own hands. Is anyone going to stop us? Who is going to protect mankind from itself? Who is going to save nature from human beings?

The person who senses the imminent approach of a catastrophe often reacts irrationally and self-destructively:

He is paralysed like a rabbit in front of a snake,
he strikes out violently at one of the guilty,
he turns away and tries to forget.

We find irrational and self-destructive attitudes like this in many people today. Resignation is on the increase. People say, 'We can't do a thing about it'. Hate is on the increase. People are looking for some scapegoat or other. Apathy is on the increase. People say, 'After us the deluge'. Where can we find the quiet courage for living and the serene yet passionate determination to do what is necessary at this moment, before it is too late?

We have God's mandate

Threatened as we are by the Flood and faced as we are by the possible annihilation of the world, let us listen to the words of the promise given to Noah:

> And God blessed Noah and his sons, and said to them,
> 'Be fruitful and multiply, and fill the earth.
> The fear of you and the dread of you
> shall be upon every beast of the earth,
> and upon every bird of the air,
> upon everything that creeps on the ground
> and all the fish of the sea;
> into your hand they are delivered.'

These words of blessing are nothing less than the renewal of human destiny – the designation to be God's image on earth, as Gen. 1.28 describes it. In the creation story, the making of man and the ordaining of human beings to be God's image on earth sounds as clear and simple as it did on the first day of creation itself. But here we are told that God renews the mandate he gave to human beings, in spite of the history of human wickedness. God remains faithful to the earth, even though he was very justly 'sorry that he had made man on the earth' when he saw 'that the wickedness of man was great in the earth, and that every imagination of the thoughts of his heart was only evil continually' (6.5f.). Here creation becomes grace – pure, undeserved grace. It was a self-humiliation on God's part when he lent his divine image to a clod of earth. But how much more God lowered himself after the Flood, in the renewal of his blessing! For he now put his glory in the hands of potential evil-doers. Men and women are again given authority to rule over the earth, even though they have spoilt everything once and can spoil it again. This is the pure, undeserved dignity we have been given. And none of us can sneak away from this responsibility for life on earth.

God has conferred his mandate to rule over world-wide creation on *human beings in general*. We find nothing about its being given to only one nation, or only one class, or only one race, or only one sex. The rights and duties of this mandate belong to all human beings and every human being. This means that people can only exercise it *together* – each according to his abilities and each according to his needs. Every kind of class domination, racial discrimination, repression of women, imperialism and dictatorship is a perversion of man's designation as God's image; and it is also a perversion of the common human mandate to rule over the earth. It is only when every single person participates to the full in the living processes of society and its political decisions that this divine mandate will be carried out. Whenever the rights and duties involved in this participation are denied to people of other nations, classes, races, religions and views, or to people of the other sex, we are called upon to resist, for God's sake.

God thinks that human beings are capable of rule – every human being, all human beings, humanity as a whole: so no one has any right to withhold this trust from other people. God thinks that human beings are capable of rule; so no one has the right to withhold confidence in this dignity and this authority from himself.

It is in conditions of wickedness and Flood that God repeats the covenant given at creation, and renews his blessing. So even in the wickedness we cause and suffer, God's covenant and human dignity remain. But what does this dominion look like?

The bitter dominion

In the creation story it all sounded innocent enough:

> Subdue the earth; and have dominion over the fish of the sea and over the birds of the air and over every living thing that moves upon the earth (Gen. 1.28).

After the Flood the same thing has a brutal sound:

> The fear of you and the dread of you shall be upon every beast of the earth . . . into your hand they are delivered (Gen. 9.2).

Can this still be called a blessing? For the human beings who want to survive, perhaps. But certainly not for the animals. Peace among created beings is a thing of the past. Now the domination of the world is linked with the threat of death. In the rest of the Old Testament we only find this rule 'through fear and dread' over the enemies who 'are given into your hand' in Israel's 'Holy Wars'. But here survival itself takes on a bitter tang. Now preservation from annihilation is only possible if the inescapability of killing is made one of the conditions of human existence. We can call this immoral or ugly if we like. At this point the blessing to human beings does in fact bring fear and dread to the animals, and the survival of the one means the death of the other. This becomes evident if we compare the economic aspect of God's covenant with Noah with the covenant given at creation.

In the creation story (Gen. 1.29f.), human beings and beasts alike are told to gain sustenance from plants. Animals are not there simply to provide food for human beings. They sit down at the same vegetarian table as men and women. But here we are told:

> Every moving thing that lives shall be food for you; and as I gave you the green plants, I give you everything. Only you shall not eat flesh with its life, that is its blood (9.3f.).

Human beings have to kill animals for food. This is certainly at variance with the peace of creation. It is bound to lead to 'fear and dread' of human beings. The blessing given by God to every living thing now includes the permission to kill. Can this still be called a blessing?

At all events the permission to kill must be restricted. People are allowed to slaughter animals for food, but they must not eat 'flesh with its life', its 'blood'. Is it blood itself that is being forbidden here? Is it living flesh that is thought of? The word blood suggests 'bloodthirstiness', the murderous desire which is all too easily given free rein through the permission to kill. So killing for the sake of food is linked with the prohibition of the lust for killing. This means that it is bound up, too, with a ban on the extermination of animal species. The 'blood' of an animal probably means both these things. Is this where we have to look for the blessing?

It must be here. For in the conditions of a creation threatened by wickedness and Flood, the transition from vegetable to animal food seemed a necessity if human beings were to survive. The myths of many peoples tell the story of this drama. So the new perils had to be guarded against. The killing of animals must not become extermination.

Today mankind has 'increased'. It has filled the earth – indeed, more than filled it. This makes food the main problem. In order to produce two pounds of meat today, ten pounds of vegetable protein are needed, apart from other feeding stuffs. This vegetable protein could contribute directly to human nourishment. If growing humanity wants to survive, the wealthy countries will have to restrict their consumption of meat and will have to distribute vegetable food justly.

This means that we are standing on the threshold of a new phase of civilization: the transition from animal to vegetarian food is important if mankind is to survive at all.

God gave the whole of mankind the food it needs – through plants first of all; then (in the covenant with Noah) through animals; and today, there is no doubt, more through plants again. He gave this food to every single person, to all human beings, to mankind as a whole. Every form of wealth acquired at the cost of other nations, and every kind of economic imperialism, debases the dignity of men and women, and is an infringement of God's glory. Economic human rights are just as inalienable a part of man's likeness to God as his right to political freedom. Anyone who disregards these rights is disregarding God.

But economic human rights inescapably involve ecological duties. Nature, animals, plants and minerals have their rights as well. Anyone who disregards the rights of the earth, 'exploiting' mineral resources and 'exterminating' animals or plants, is an evildoer and an agent of the Flood. God has a passionate interest in the nourishment of men and women. Anyone who thinks that, when all is said and done, these are merely primitive needs and have nothing to do with religion, is at liberty to pursue his higher interests all by himself. God's interests are something he has failed to comprehend. Religion begins with eating. Eating is a religious activity, in both the Old and the New Testaments. That is why the 'menus' play so important a part in salvation history.

In the prehistoric times our story is talking about, the transition from vegetarian to animal food was mankind's fundamental problem. It was the fundamental problem because it led to the killing of living things.

Today, for reasons of humanity, the transition from animal to vegetarian food is the main economic problem, because vegetarian food can feed more people. But could this transition not also be a way of mitigating and resolving the bitterness of killing in order to eat and survive?

Thou shalt not kill!

In the conditions of wickedness and Flood under which they are living, God has to protect men and women. He has to protect them especially from themselves and from their fellow human beings. Almost all animals have the instinct to preserve their own species. They do not kill and devour beings like themselves. Only human beings lack this protective instinct. Killing their own species is a typical and almost exclusively human act. That is why there has to be an apodictic divine command to protect human beings from themselves:

> For your lifeblood I will surely require a reckoning;
> of every beast I will require it,
> and of man I will require the life of man,
> for he is your brother.
> Whoever sheds the blood of man,
> by man shall his blood be shed;
> for God made man in his own image (9.5f.).

The blood is a person's life, so it belongs to God. But the person is not merely God's property; he is also God's image, his representative and his glory on earth. That is why God has to 'require' any human blood that is shed.

Human beings are forbidden to shed human blood: that is the absolute prohibition. Anyone who kills another person is committing fratricide. The wickedness that once upon a time led to the Flood began with the murder of Abel by his brother Cain. Significantly enough, it was fratricide that started the deadly history of the struggle for supremacy. The murderer was Abel's brother, not his sister. It was the man who succumbed to this temptation, not the woman. It was with the struggle for domination that historically speaking the suppression of the woman began. 'Men make history', we have been told ever since – and that is just what history looks like. That is why the divine commandment 'Thou shalt not kill' is directed here in the first instance to the man. God will expiate the murder of every single person 'as if he were his brother'. We must not immediately generalize this specific reference to the man. It is we men who belong to the race of Cain, not women.

But anyone who kills another human being murders God too. The murder of a human being destroys God's image and God's child, so murder is the thing that is absolutely forbidden. The murderer robs God of his image on earth. The murderer violates God's love for his beloved child. That is why he comes into conflict with God himself. God himself is struck to the heart when one human being kills another. He therefore has to 'require' the blood himself. Because he is faithful to his image and his covenant, God has to expiate the murder. The blood that has been shed 'cries out to high heaven'. But in what way does God protect his earthly image? We find the answer in the classic principle:

Whoever sheds the blood of man,
by man shall his blood be shed (9.6).

Is this a proverb, or a legal maxim, or a prophetic warning? The sentence sounds very like the saying of Jesus:

For all who take the sword
will perish by the sword (Matt. 26.52).

Some interpreters think that the Old Testament statement justifies the death penalty for murder, and provides the foundation for it. But up to now no one has ever imagined that Jesus' saying is a justification for the death penalty – on the contrary. For when Jesus was taken prisoner in Gethsemane he linked this statement of a general truth with his demand to Peter: 'Put your sword back into its place.' For Jesus this statement means the renunciation of violence. Can we possibly suppose that in the covenant with Noah the maxim really means anything different? God alone is the avenger: '*I* will require. . .' he says. Nothing whatsoever is said about transferring this right to human beings. 'Whoever sheds the blood of man, by man shall his blood be shed.' That is the description of a fact and the inescapable result of an act. If the shedding of human blood is really absolutely forbidden to human beings – forbidden in the name of God – then the death penalty becomes preposterous too. Bloodshed does not prevent bloodshed. It simply breeds it. The divine protection of the human life that is imperilled by other human beings can, in history, take the form of the death penalty, as a kind of emergency measure of self-defence. But the divine protection is itself really called in question by any such measure. The person who is endangered is not safeguarded by the death penalty – on the contrary. God's right

to the life of human beings remains, and so does his right to 'require'
the life of which he has been robbed. This is what the story makes
unequivocally plain.

Hope as the direction of the covenant

At the end of the story, God's faithfulness is described in a picture of
supreme poetic beauty:

> I set my bow in the cloud,
> and it shall be a sign of the covenant between me and the earth.
> When I bring clouds over the earth
> and the bow is seen in the clouds,
> I will remember my covenant
> which is between me and you and every living creature of all flesh;
> and the waters shall never again become a flood
> to destroy all flesh (9.13–15).

Against the dark and threatening clouds of the coming annihilation,
the rainbow appears as a token: as a reminder to God, a recollection
of his promise; and as a sign of hope for the frightened people, so that
they may commit themselves and their children in confidence to the
faithfulness of their God.

The promise never again to destroy all flesh because of its wickedness is an unconditional promise on God's part. It is God's indestructible 'Yes' to his creation. The history of nature, with its changes
and chances, and the uncertain history of humanity, both rest on the
foundation of God's unconditional will. Natural catastrophes and
the human catastrophes of history cannot annul this divine 'Yes' to
creation and to the human person. Not even human wickedness can
thwart the creator's will towards his creation. God remains true to
the earth, for God remains true to himself. He cannot deny himself.

What does this mean for God? It means an infinite readiness for
suffering. God has to endure wickedness on earth without avenging
the deed or annihilating the doer of it. He has to wait, as the Father
of the Prodigal Son waited, until the son turns back. In infinite
patience he has to woo human beings to this new beginning. The
unbounded suffering of the divine love is the concrete form of God's
faithfulness to the earth. And in the image of 'the Lamb slain from
the foundation of the world' we know the price that has to be paid

for this divine faithfulness, the faithfulness of the God from whom everything lives that has breath.

What does this mean for us? It means that in spite of all our justifiable mistrust in human history and the history of nature, our fundamental confidence in reality can be greater still. Reality in its deepest foundations is worthy of trust, for it is good. In the abyss of our disappointments we find God's hope. In the deepest depths of appalling guilt we find God's grace. In the bitterness of suffering that offers no escape we find God's love. At the heart of everything is God's unswerving 'Yes'. And God stands firm.

Today we need this confidence in the future more than ever before: as a confidence made wise by experience; as a confidence which does not destroy itself. For confidence allows us to be clear-headed, and to overcome the resignation, the hate and the apathy that threaten us. Trust like this gives us the serene and steadfast passion which allows us to do resolutely whatever is required of us here and now, so that our children and the children of all the peoples on earth can live in peace.

God's promise, 'I will never again curse the earth', gives us all the chance to live.

2 The Calling of the Unworthy

But Moses said to the Lord, 'Oh, my Lord, I am not eloquent, either heretofore or since thou hast spoken to thy servant; but I am slow of speech and of tongue.' Then the Lord said to him, 'Who has made man's mouth? Who makes him dumb, or deaf, or seeing, or blind? Is it not I, the Lord? Now therefore go, and I will be with your mouth and teach you what you shall speak.' But he said, 'Oh, my Lord, send, I pray, some other person.' Then the anger of the Lord was kindled against Moses and he said, 'Is there not Aaron, your brother, the Levite? I know that he can speak well; and behold, he is coming out to meet you, and when he sees you he will be glad in his heart. And you shall speak to him and put the words in his mouth; and I will be with your mouth and with his mouth, and will teach you what you shall do. He shall speak for you to the people; and he shall be a mouth for you, and you shall be to him as God' (Exodus 4.10–16).

This chapter comes between Moses' miraculous call on Mount Horeb and the beginning of his glorious liberation of his people from slavery in Egypt. It is an unfamiliar chapter in the story of Moses – no more than a little private entr'acte in the great liberation drama. To put it bluntly from the outset, it is an embarrassing and irritating episode. The bards of world literature usually draw a tactful veil over weaknesses of this kind. So if anybody is looking for heroes in the struggle for emancipation and liberty (either because he would like to be a hero himself, or just because he would rather pass the job on to someone else), he would do better to stop listening at this point and look elsewhere.

I will freely admit that I was disappointed when I re-read this chapter. I was disappointed in Moses. My picture of him was different. When we were children we had a beautiful illustrated Bible at home, in which Moses looked like God the Father in person, or as my own father sometimes looked: tall and imposing, ponderous with the weight of authority, awesome, just, but always strict, always dramatic in pose. This was the way Michelangelo immortalized him in stone: muscular, mightily bearded, his eyes fixed on eternity, with tables of the law for an intractable people and punishments to hand for naughty children – a superman from Sinai. Even Freud was impressed. He analysed his father-complex and wrote a book which he called *Der Mann Mose* (in English, *Moses and Monotheism*). Moses – the name reaches back to childhood fears. For us, Moses stood for the God who is always to be dreaded but seldom loved. The whole power of the commandments depended on his authority.

But the peoples who are oppressed, the unemployed in the slums of Sao Paulo, the evicted labourers in North Brazil, the men and women suffering discrimination in South Africa – all these people have a very different picture of Moses. For them his name sounds like that of Marx or Mao. They are suffering oppression today as the children of Israel once did during the building of the pyramids. They are crying out for deliverance. They are hungering for life. They are waiting for their liberation. They are ready for the exodus, and for the long march to a better future. For these people, Moses is the prototype of hope. 'Go down, Moses' and 'Let my people go'. The spirituals sung by the black slaves in the cotton fields of the southern states of North America see Moses like that. He is the freedom fighter, the fearless deliverer. For people who are oppressed, all the Bible's hopes crystallize in the expectation of a new Moses. The name Moses stands for liberty.

But whichever picture of Moses we have in our mind's eye – the picture of oppressive authority, or the picture of the guide to freedom – this chapter destroys them both. There he stands, this hole-picking grouser, with his endless new objections; this drip, with his self-pity and his continual whining at the God of hope, calling in question the whole liberation of his people through his excuses.

Just before I sat my university entrance exam in the last year of the war, 1944–45, commissions went from school to school, looking for boys who were willing and able to fight. We called them 'heropinchers', and plenty of people got the necessary excuses ready, so as to save their skins. In spite of the obvious differences, this is what this incident between Moses and his God reminds me of. Moses does not want to be a prophet. He is absolutely determined not to be a hero. And the Lord has to conjure up ideas in plenty before he can turn this mulish farm worker into the leader of national liberation.

This Moses is certainly not Michelangelo's superman. And he does not resemble the great liberators of the nations either. He is merely a shepherd without any possessions, a poor old man who wants to be left in peace, and not to have anything to do with the insane demands his Lord proposes to make on him. And when it really comes to the point, he is a hard-boiled egoist, for whom hope is no principle at all. This is the lamentable creature with whom the Lord is going to bring about his revolution, lead his people to freedom and create salvation for the nations!

Let us look at the story closely, and try to see it with the eyes of the imprisoned and the ears of the oppressed – which means with the eyes and ears of the children of Israel in Moses' time, and the wretched people in Africa and Latin America today. What impression does the story make, if we read it with the desolate eyes of the slum-dwellers?

The Lord is full of hope, but Moses is a realist. 'No one will believe me,' he says. 'Behold, they will not believe me or listen to my voice, for they will say, "The Lord did not appear to you" ' (4.1). That is his first objection, and it is a good one. He knows his brothers. They are a sceptical people. He will have to produce more than a mere assertion about what God has said, with himself as witness. How, after all, are his countrymen supposed to know whether the Lord has really appeared to him? How are they supposed to discern that the Lord from Sinai has 'a strong hand' and can really do what he promises them?

But according to the story Moses' problem is not a problem for almighty God at all. Moses is given not merely *one* magic power. He is given two at once. He can change his staff into a snake. With his own hand he can make people sick and well again, as he likes. And in case of emergencies, he is even given a *third* gift: he can turn water into blood. The Lord is absolutely confident: 'If they will not believe you, or heed the first sign, they may believe the latter sign.' And if they still do not believe after they have seen the second sign, then there is the third one, to be used in case of need. And it is true – the

Lord is quite right. This is just the way things turn out with the children of Israel. At the end of the chapter we read: 'And when they heard that the Lord had visited the people of Israel and that he had seen their affliction, they bowed their heads and worshipped' (4.31). According to this, the people were convinced more by what they heard than by the magic. But let us go back to Moses.

When he pointed out that the Israelites were an unbelieving, sceptical people, it was only a red herring. It is he himself who is sceptical about the whole affair. This encounter with God is an embarrassment to him. He would like to get rid of his tremendous vocation. After his sociological excuses, 'Who am I, after all?' and, 'No one will believe me', he now comes up with a psychological one: he is a poor speaker. He stutters. He is handicapped. We know that it is probably some early psychological damage, a disturbed relationship with the mother, which makes itself felt in this unpleasant way: 'I am slow of speech and of tongue' (4.10). It must also be said that Moses becomes slightly impudent at this point. He lets the Lord God know at once that his tiresome speech-defect has not improved at all, even after this miraculous divine encounter: 'I am not eloquent, either heretofore or since thou hast spoken to thy servant.'

But for Almighty God this is not a problem either: 'Who has made man's mouth. . . ? Now therefore go, and I will be with your mouth and teach you what you shall speak.' This is exactly the way that Jesus strengthens the trust of his disciples: when they accuse you, when they torture you and use violence to make you talk, then, 'Take no thought how or what you shall speak: for it shall be given you in that same hour what you shall speak. For it is not you that speak, but the Spirit of your Father which speaks through you' (Matt. 10.19f.). So the trust in God to which the Lord calls Moses sweeps aside both sociology and psychology. What is left?

What is left is Moses, all by himself, naked, without any way of escape, without excuses, without any hiding place. Now he has to decide. He has put his objections. They have been demolished. Now Moses refuses altogether. 'Lord, send some other person.' Please, anyone but me. Then Moses breaks off his negotiations with the Lord.

But he cannot get rid of this Lord, or his calling. In his wrath and his wounded love, the Lord does not make things easier for Moses. He makes them more difficult. Instead of curing his speech defect by means of another miracle, he sends Moses into the battle with his 'slow tongue', merely giving him Aaron, a Levite, to be with him as interpreter. 'He shall speak for you to the people; and he shall be a mouth for you, and you shall be to him as God.' But God makes things more difficult for himself in this way, too. He does not want to visit his people in their misery and lead them out of slavery into freedom by means of some mighty wonder or by the gift of miraculous speech. He wants to fulfil his purpose by way of this curious team, Moses and Aaron, a poor shepherd and an ageing priest; one of them with a 'slow tongue', the other who has first of all to interpret the incomprehensible message; one of them eighty years old and the other eighty-three. God's prophet is given a second prophet as companion, and God's proxy another proxy of his own. The series of mediations between God and man becomes longer than was originally envisaged. How many sources of error are there in this transmission from mouth to mouth, with a slow tongue?

Yet this is the beginning of the people's liberation. For all we hear about Moses after this is that he went away in silence (4.18). Calling is election; this election is nomination; this nomination is a destiny which does not enquire about the sociological and psychological circumstances. Moses is not free to refuse. He accepts the fact that he had been condemned to let his speech-defect be made good by his brother Aaron. 'And Moses went.' The Lord is determined to have his way in spite of Moses' objections. He is going to have his way even though Moses is so unwilling. Moses understands and falls silent. It is here that his greatness begins. He has tried to resist his destiny in every possible way. His excellent sociological and psychological arguments have not helped him, neither has his flat 'no'. So he gives way to the force which is stronger than himself. His obstinacy is broken. In everything he says and does he has to trust in the Lord alone. For Moses, God has become irresistible. As a result Moses becomes ruthless towards himself and his people too, and even more so towards the mighty Pharaoh.

If we try to see this story through the eyes of the imprisoned Israelites, it does not take much imagination to picture the impatience the groaning slaves must have felt if they knew how difficult their liberator was making things for the Lord. Does the chosen person have to be so feeble, so speechless, so devious and, if we come down to it, so uninterested? If we put ourselves in the place of the men and women who were hungering for freedom and waiting for their liberator, then their initial reaction was probably: if we have to depend on a wash-out like this, we shall never be free. The Lord would have done better to look for someone else – a type like Joshua or David, a *man* at least, someone with strength, courage and good will, not this ageing, handicapped shepherd from the desert, who is not even willing to take on the job.

Anyone who is imprisoned and condemned to forced labour, anyone who is oppressed and always hungry, often dreams of the person who will set him free. One day the supreme divine power will descend on the evil forces at the camp gates and on the soldiers on the watch towers, with their machine guns. Then the gates will open and one will walk out into freedom. The trumpet announces the saviour, as it does in Beethoven's *Fidelio*. The one 'who comes in the name of the Lord' will appear in a blaze of light. The dreams of the powerless are beautiful dreams. But the real story of Moses and Israel's exodus ran quite differently. It was human, earthly. So we ought really to ask: when – later on – the people who had once been liberated told their children the story of the exodus, why did they report this embarrassing little interlude in the drama, since this, after all, was a purely private affair? Why did they not touch up the picture a little, like the illustrated Bible, or turn Moses into a hero like Michelangelo? Why did they think it was important to tell their children about the great liberator's ugly little weaknesses?

The first reason is initially quite simple. The cult of the individual, the deification of persons, was forbidden in Israel. It was not Moses who led the children of Israel to freedom; it was the Lord, and the Lord alone. Certainly *through* Moses, just as Moses spoke through Aaron, but basically in spite of him, and in spite of all the forms of resistance he could conjure up. When we read the biographies of the great national liberators, the heroes and helpers of mankind, we do not find any trace of the anti-hero attitude the Israelites show here.

The second reason is that the Lord does not liberate people through miracles of power and eloquence or any other conjuring tricks which really paralyse the liberty of human beings. He frees people through people, with all their handicaps, with their signs of age and their disabilities. This is comforting, but not only that: it is salutary as well. This brings the helpless and the prisoners down to earth again – back from their visions of power, back from their delirium, away from their dreams of revenge, away from the unrealistic radicalism which is afraid of contact with reality. Moses is like you and me. Liberation comes on limping, human feet, for it is liberation by the human God and not by inhuman idols. So at the Passover supper, whoever tells his children about the glorious exodus of his fathers from slavery into the promised land of liberty also has to tell this story about the human, all-too-human Moses.

Of course in retrospect Israel can remember the splendour of the exodus in conjunction with the inadequacy of Moses. Later this honest realism does not present so many problems. But how does it sound to people who have no hope, who have been robbed of their future, to the people in the Third World who have been reduced to silence? I cannot speak for the poor. But I do know that everyone who realizes how strong oppression is, because he himself shares the helplessness of the people, can understand Moses and his resistance very well indeed. Anyone who has to oppose a military junta, anyone who has to change the structures of injustice, anyone who has to resist the mass pressure of fear and denunciation, will mobilize anything and everything to avoid having to take a stand: the sociological reasons (the people will not believe me; they are too apathetic) and the psychological ones (whether one is eloquent or not, what use are words and language against acts of brutal violence?). And there is the personal refusal, too: send some other person. It is only when all these reasons, objections and refusals have been struck out of a person's hand because the Lord himself has become his destiny that he can take up his task. Then there is only this one thing: the liberty of the people. Everything else is in the hand of almighty God. Anyone who arrives at this point acquires the staying-power of hope. Kafka's writings are often profoundly sad, but he puts it like this:

> The premonition of final liberation is not disproved because next day the imprisonment is still unchanged, or even intensified, or even if one is explicitly told that the imprisonment is never to end. On the contrary, all this can be the very precondition that is necessary for the final liberation.

The person for whom God himself becomes destiny discovers this enduring hope.

3   Openness for the Coming God

The earth is the Lord's and the fullness thereof, the world and those who dwell therein;
for he has founded it upon the seas, and established it upon the rivers.
Who shall ascend the hill of the Lord? and who shall stand in his holy place?
He who has clean hands and a pure heart, who does not lift up his soul to what is false, and does not swear deceitfully.
He will receive blessing from the Lord, and righteousness from the God of his salvation.
Such is the generation of those who seek him, who seek the face of the God of Jacob.
Lift up your heads, O gates! and be lifted up, you doors in the world, that the King of glory may come in.
Who is this King of glory? The Lord, strong and mighty, the Lord, mighty in battle!
Lift up your heads, O gates! and be lifted up, you doors in the world, that the King of glory may come in.
Who is this King of glory? The Lord of hosts, he is the King of glory (Psalm 24).

Prayer
You come to us, O Lord. Into our poverty comes your wealth.
Into our emptiness comes your fullness. Into our ugliness comes your beauty.
Make us ready to open ourselves to you. Break down the walls behind which we hide ourselves. Quench the fear that burns in us, and our shame before you.

You come, and make us rich and great and lovely.
Come, Lord, come soon.

Advent in early Israel – Advent in our world of today: it is a long road
from one to the other. But the road leads in the same direction and
with an ever deeper and wider hope. The Lord of glory is coming.
The closed doors and the barricaded gates are to open to him now,
today. He brings with him the new human being, with innocent
hands and a pure heart. The people who enquire about God and seek
his face will receive blessing and righteousness from the God of
salvation.

The world and those who dwell in it will sigh with relief, for the
divine beauty will fill everything through and through. Or, to put it
in a different way: this earth is the Lord's. It has not been given up to
itself, or to us human beings either. Its Creator is coming to glorify it.
The people who live in it have not been forsaken. They will not perish
from their injustice or be destroyed in their guilt. Their Creator is
coming to find them and to rejoice with them.

This is a festal hymn and a great song. Let us try to praise the
coming glory, in the face of the threats hanging over our world; let us
try to love its beauty, in spite of the ugly things men and women do
to one another; let us try to throw open for this future the inward and
outward doors behind which we have hidden ourselves. God himself
is coming to meet his creation, and when men and women come to
meet him in creative receptivity, they can become free and lovely and
lovable.

Advent in early Israel. Psalm 24 probably dates from Israel's early
struggles and victories after the settlement in Palestine. These are
fragments and antiphons taken from what is called a 'gate liturgy'.
Yahweh Sabaoth, the Lord of the heavenly hosts and of Israel's
earthly armies, is invisibly enthroned upon the ark of the covenant.
During their campaigns Israel's warriors carried this ark into battle
with them, so that Yahweh Sabaoth might confuse the enemy with
'holy fear' and help his own people to victory. The ark was the visible
throne of the invisible God, and to know that it was with them gave
the people courage and confidence: God is with us – come what may!
After the victory the ark was taken back to the sanctuary. This may

have been both a priestly procession and a military parade, celebrating Yahweh's 'war heroes' and all the lesser heroes in Israel.

When the ark arrived at Zion, there was a ceremonial game of question and answer between the arrivals and the people who were awaiting them: 'Who shall ascend the hill of the Lord and stand in his holy place? He who has clean hands. Who is the Lord of glory? It is the Lord of hosts, strong and mighty in battle. Open the gates wide and lift up the doors, that the Lord of glory may come in.' Then the procession moved into the holy city and the great celebration began. 'Advent in early Israel' was certainly the glorious entry of Yahweh, 'the war hero'. We can be sure that nothing was lacking in the feast they celebrated. One can imagine it so easily, because the nations have always celebrated their victories with this mixture of religion and politics. Our people, too, once had a God who 'made iron grow' and 'knew no slaves'. So we have hardly come here today simply to be reminded of Israel's divine 'war hero'. But there is more to Psalm 24 than this; and Yahweh Sabaoth is more than simply a minor Middle East military hero. 'The earth is the Lord's and all who dwell therein.' This God of Israel is not Israel's private God. He is the creator of everything that exists. And he does not fight to destroy. He fights to preserve the earth and to make it habitable, in the face of all the forces of annihilation.

'The Lord Sabaoth is the Lord of glory.' This God is not merely Israel's war hero. He comes to fill all the countries of the world with the splendour of his glory, and to bless all nations with his righteousness.

Yahweh Sabaoth is therefore a God full of potentiality. As the beginning and the end of the psalm makes clear, faith in him spreads the open hands of his hope over the whole world, in expectation of its all-embracing glorification. This is not summed up by any minor victory procession in early Israel. It goes further than that.

Advent in our world of today. What has happened to the world we live in? At the time when the psalm was written, human beings were small, and nature was great and mysterious. In the sands of the desert, the storms, the times of drought and the periods of flood, nature was not subject to human beings; human beings were at the mercy of nature. As a result, petty humanity saw sinister gods and demons at work in the mighty forces of nature. And yet Israel acknowledged

Yahweh as creator, trusted in the goodness of his creation, and did not allow itself to be intimidated.

For us, things have been reversed. The earth is man's and the world, too. We have investigated nature and subjugated it. We have overpopulated the earth and are now doubtful whether our children are going to find it habitable at all. This is just as sinister, for we no longer trust human beings – these new gods and demons who rule over nature. So today we need just as much courage as people did long ago, if we are to confess God as creator in the face of the destruction of the environment and the ecological crisis, if we are to trust in the goodness of his creation, if we are not to be intimidated by our fear of catastrophe but are to do in time what has to be done. The earth is the Lord's. Today this trust has to be supported more than ever by the hope that he will come to glorify himself in that earth and the earth in him.

This means that for us the second point becomes all the more important: who shall ascend the hill of the Lord? In other words, who is going to share in the coming glory? Who are the children of the future, the children of peace? Psalm 24 evidently knew people who had clean hands and pure hearts, people who enquired about God and sought his face. But our hands are not clean. Our hearts are not pure. If we enquire about anything, it is usually about ourselves, and if we seek something, it is generally our own face and our own glory. The earth has certainly become the world of human beings, but human beings have not become any more humane in the process. How do we become human in the true sense? How do we become people with 'blessing and righteousness from the God of salvation', as the psalm puts it? The victors of those early times, who subjugated their enemies, were not people like that. And the cold, hard managers and technocrats who control nature, the economy and our whole society today are certainly not people like that either. So what are we waiting for in this present Advent? Who are we waiting for? And what expectation colours our lives, our sufferings and our actions?

The psalm reminds us of the feast of joy with which Israel celebrated the entry of the victorious Lord Sabaoth. For us this is a picture to remind us of a broader and deeper hope: the feast of the coming Lord of glory in the whole world. His glory will not be the glory of victory, and the triumph over the enemies that have been defeated. It will be the glory of peace, and triumph over the enmity that has been overcome. The prophets already transformed the image that reminded people of Yahweh of hosts, and spread a different hope: 'Rejoice greatly, O daughter of Zion! Shout aloud, O daughter of Jerusalem! Lo, your king comes to you; he is just and a helper, humble and riding on an ass. For I will cut off the chariots from Ephraim and the war horses from Jerusalem, and the battle bow shall be broken: for he will teach peace to the nations, and his dominion shall be to the ends of the earth' (Zech. 9.9f.).

This is no longer the glory of victory, it is the splendour of peace. It is no longer the power of panzers and rockets, it is the force of help. This is no longer the love of power, it is the power of love. This is not the riches that make many poor, but the poverty of God which makes many rich. Anyone who hopes for the future of this Lord – poor, and riding upon an ass – does not himself become strong in performance and achievement, or mighty in the competitive struggle. He becomes receptive in love, open in participation, and vulnerable in community and fellowship.

This is the image of a hope for an experience which is wider and deeper even than that. From earliest times the Christian community used Psalm 24 as an Advent hymn which reflected its experience with Christ, because in Yahweh Sabaoth they rediscovered the Father of Jesus Christ. Indeed Luther actually saw Yahweh Sabaoth in Christ himself, as his hymn shows:

> Ask ye who is this same?
> Christ Jesus is his name,
> The Lord Sabaoth
> And no other God
> Shall conquer in the battle.

And Paul too called the risen Christ the Lord of glory.

This modifies the psalm's reminder and the prophet's hope yet again. For Christ did not come to conquer and to rule, but *to serve*. His victory was his surrender of himself to death on the cross 'as a ransom for many'. His lordship does not make a slave of anyone, but lies in his becoming a slave for the liberation of many others. His riches are to be found in the very fact that he becomes poor in order to make many others rich. The Son of man does not rule through acts of violence and subjugation, but through the giving of himself for the liberation of men and women. We can hardly conceive of a more radical revolution in the idea of rule than the coming of Christ as it is experienced here: the only Lord – a servant of all; the ruler of worlds – a friend of sinners and tax collectors; the universal judge – the brother of the outcasts.

This changes our whole concept of glory, greatness, achievement, and the development of power. Normally we look upwards, to someone above us, when we are impressed by his glory. But in the case of Jesus we have to look *downwards*. We discover his glory in his humbleness, his greatness in his poverty, his power in his self-surrender, from the wretched manger in Bethlehem to the desolate cross on Golgotha.

The lords of this earth surround themselves with all the splendour of wealth; people who are highly respected receive honour; teachers clothe themselves in authority; and the nations strive for military glory. But 'the Lord of glory' shows his strength in the weak and his honour in his surrender and his joy in his love. We should really try to stop thinking of glory simply in terms of rule. We should add the idea of beauty, too. People are supposed to obey a ruler. But beauty confers joy and allows a person to grow and develop. The person and history of Christ manifests the beauty of God's love, the love which empties itself without losing itself, which can forgive without being untrue to itself. God is beauty, and he is nowhere lovelier than in the winning tenderness and the prevenient grace which comes to meet us in Christ. If we can hope with complete assurance that the future of the world's life is the beauty of his grace and the glory of his liberating love, then our hearts will be enlarged, as the psalmist puts it, and our shut-in world will be thrown open. We shall again become open people, creatively alive, without reservations and without securities. We can give ourselves entirely and without division, just as he gave himself entirely to us.

Let me add here a critical word about our present situation. Why do we subject our school children and students to such pressure? The pressure to produce 'results' and the need to compete for places at university, and for jobs? We are shutting out the weak and preventing even the strong from developing their more human characteristics. Why do we violate nature and ourselves because of a greed for power which – as we all know – can be fatal? Why do we build one kind of security after another into our society, so as to make all our institutions unassailable and invulnerable? Is it not fear that is behind all this – pure existential fear, fear for our property and dread of the claims of other people? Is it not based on an aggressiveness without joy, which is prepared to let others suffer? We all know the many reasons for this development. But its many results are perhaps less well known. Because we are afraid of other people we shut one door after another on our own future. We prevent other people from developing, and the characteristics we ourselves develop in the process are not precisely our most attractive ones. We do not want to give our enemies a chance; and so we spoil our own chances. The things in us which say 'yes' to life get left behind: feeling, spontaneous affection, brotherliness, and joy in existence.

Advent now: 'Lift up your heads, O gates! and be lifted up, you doors in the world!' This surely means a counter-movement to closed-in men and women and closed societies, a movement of openness for others and for one another, out of confidence in the open future of God of which no one has to be afraid.

'Who shall ascend the hill of the Lord and stand in his holy place?' asks the psalm. Let us look at our hands. They are not clean. They were clenched when they should have been open. They fended off when they might have invited. They seized and snatched when they should have given. They struck, shot, condemned, took possession and neglected many things. Advent now: the expectation of Christ's coming and the beauty of his grace. Our hands are not clean and we cannot wash them in innocence. But we can open our guilty, fearful hands, just as they are, and receive the beauty of his grace. Advent now: the expectation of Christ's coming. We can unclose our clenched fists and give what we have, and share what we have gathered to ourselves, and open our hands for the gift of the nearness of God. It is not what we have achieved that counts, nor what we possess. The only thing that counts is the beauty of the coming God, because it sustains us and makes the earth a place fit to live in.

Let us look at our hearts. They can hardly be called pure. They are divided, torn hither and thither. They are full of fear and aggression. That is why we do not know what we live by and what we ought to do. We are confused. That is why we do not see God. We do not love with our whole hearts, and do not seek God with our whole hearts. With us everything is half-hearted and divided. We accuse ourselves – and defend ourselves. And the worst thing of all is that when our hearts accuse us, we no longer know that God is greater than our hearts. That is why we continually reproach ourselves and other people.

Advent now: the expectation of Christ's coming. We can open our hearts, so that they will be pure in the beauty of the Lord, and steadfast in hope, and joyful in his feast. 'Blessed are the pure in heart, for they shall see God,' we are told. But the reverse is true, too: the person who looks on God in Christ receives a pure heart.

So who shall ascend the hill of the Lord? I should like to read the psalm differently. It is the person who has guilty hands and is grasped by the outstretched hands of Christ who will ascend that hill. Who will stand in his holy place? I should like to answer that it is the person with an impure heart which has become clear and joyful in the beauty of Christ's grace who can stand the test. Who are the children of the future? I should like to answer: the people who renounce domination and the dreams of rule, people who are not victorious and do not dream of victories, but who open themselves and their institutions in creative receptivity towards what is divine, towards what is human, and towards what is natural. These people are the heirs of his future.

Lift up your heads, O gates – so that the Lord of glory may come in, with grace for the people who ask it, and beauty for the ugly. Open the doors in the world, in this city, this university, this society, so that the Lord of glory may enter, with justice for all and peace for everyone. Open hearts like this are beautiful, and open societies are lovely. They make life vital, receptive and expectant. They make the earth habitable. But they are costly. The person who lays himself open becomes vulnerable. The person who trusts can be disappointed. An open society has to live and let live, with its enemies too. But to close ourselves to others in hardness of heart, and to live with clenched fists, would surely mean not living at all any more. It would mean being buried alive. A closed society would be a dead society, without any future. It would merely spread death and would die itself, of its own accord. It would certainly have no enemies, but neither would it have any friends. The openness of love and the expansiveness of trust are the loveliest things in life when we meet them and when we can give them. They are possibilities which are already open to us and which have already been granted to us through the beauty of the coming God, who in his passion took the wounds, pains and disappointments of love on himself, in order to open us for his future. He draws us out of the jaws of fear into a broad place where there is no cramping.

Who is the king of glory?

He is the Lord, strong in his love and mighty in his self-giving, the Lord, lovely in the way he comes to meet us. His beauty will redeem the world.

4 The Disarming Child

The people who walked in darkness have seen a great light; those who dwelt in a land of deep darkness, on them has light shined. Thou hast multiplied the jubilation; thou hast made great the joy. The people will rejoice before thee as with joy at the harvest, as men rejoice when they divide the spoil. For the yoke of their burden and the staff on their shoulder and the rod of their oppressor thou hast broken as on the day of Midian. For every boot of the tramping warrior in battle tumult and every garment rolled in blood will be burned as fuel for the fire. For to us a child is born, to us a son is given; and the government will be upon his shoulder, and his name will be called 'Wonderful Counsellor, Mighty Hero, Everlasting Father, Prince of Peace'. Of the increase of his government and of peace there will be no end, upon the throne of David, and over his kingdom, to establish it and to uphold it with justice and righteousness from this time forth and for evermore. The zeal of the Lord of hosts will do this (Isa. 9.2–7).

Prayer
Heavenly Father, we come to you with bound hands and ask you for the joy of liberty. We stand before you entangled in our guilt and ask for the right of grace. We are wandering, lost in darkness. Each of us wants to have his own way. Lead us into the light of your presence and show us the common way of peace. You sent your son into our confused world. To us the child of peace has been born. In life and in death hold us fast in his fellowship.

This mighty vision of the prophet is founded on the liberation of oppressed men and women through the disarming birth of the divine child. Its goal is the turn from bloody war to the peace that endures and is unbroken. And in order to portray this hope for liberation and peace, the prophet falls back on a picture which is positively expressionist in style. The images jostle and tumble over one another, distorted beyond any possible reality into what is impossible for human beings – possible only to God.

The sky becomes light over the people in darkness. The light comes like the daybreak over the mountains into the land of shadows. It comes as unexpectedly as a flash of lightning in the night. Then the yoke of the enslaved will be broken, their chains will be rent apart, the truncheons of their task-masters will be snapped in two. The army boots, with their even tramp, and the bloodstained coats of the murderers will be thrown into the bonfire of peace. The groaning people are seized by jubilation which is no longer dimmed by tears. For peace is coming – peace without end. Justice is coming – justice that will never again be infringed. The kingdom is coming – the kingdom of freedom without any more earthly masters and slaves.

How does this happen? Who makes it happen? Where does it begin? And to whom does it apply? The prophet proclaims everything he sees and hopes for in the language of assurance, as if it were already present. It all tends towards a single centre, the unique event, the final reversal of everything, a reversal which can actually happen to us. 'For to us a child is born, to us a son is given. The government is upon his shoulder.'

Realistically though the prophet talks about hunger, slavery and occupying troops, he ends messianically. He lets his vision of the birth of the child and the appearance of the peace of God shine like a light into the conflicts and experiences of real life.

It is not easy to keep these dimensions together when one is used to splitting up faith and politics, God and experience, and when one is accustomed to celebrate Christmas only in the heart and in the bosom of one's own family. But the message of the prophet is a realistic vision, and what it talks about is a visionary reality. It is a message for the people, a message sent into the camps of the exiled, and into the slums of the poor. It is a word against the captains of the arms industry and the fanatics of power. If we really understand what it means, it bursts the bonds of Sunday worship in this noble church.

For if this message really lays hold of us, it leads us to Jesus the liberator, and to the people who live in darkness and who are waiting for him – and for us.

Anyone who belongs to the people who dwell in the land of darkness, or anyone who has ever belonged to it, will find this message about the disarming birth of the child as alluring as it is unbelievable. The people in deep darkness: whom does this mean? In the prophet's time it was that section of Israel which had fallen under Assyrian dictatorship. Every imprisoned Israelite knew the tramp of the invading boots, the bloody coats and the rods of the slave-drivers. Today we can still see Assyrian warriors and overseers like this in the frescoes, with their iron shoes, their cloaks and their sticks. But for the prophet, Assyria is more than just Assyria. She is the representative of the power that is hostile to God, and this makes her at the same time the very quintessence of all inhuman oppression. The prophet looks at the specific plight of his people, but talks about a misery experienced by people everywhere. That is why his words and images are so wide open that prisoners in every age have been able to find in them their own fate and their own hope.

A people in darkness: Isaiah 8 tells us what this means: 'They will pass through the land, greatly distressed and hungry; and when they are hungry, they will be enraged and will curse their king and their God, and they will stare up to the sky and look down to the earth, and will find only distress and darkness; for they are in the darkness of fear and wander lost in the darkness. God has hidden his face from them. But instead of waiting for his light, they run to fortune-tellers and mediums, and become more and more confused.

A people in darkness: let me add a personal word here. This phrase touched me directly when in 1945 we were driven in endless and desolate columns into the prisoner-of-war camps, the sticks of the guards at our sides, with hungry stomachs and empty hearts and curses on our lips. But many of us then, and I was one, glimpsed the light that radiates from the divine child. This light did not allow me to perish. This hope kept us alive.

A people in darkness: today I see before me the millions of the imprisoned, the exiled, the deported, the tortured and the silenced everywhere in the world where people are pushed into this darkness. The important point is not the nations which can be accused of these things. What is important is the world-wide brotherhood of the men and women who are living in darkness. For it is on them that this divine light now shines.

A people in darkness: how that cries out today from the Third World in Africa and Asia, and from the Third World in our own country – cries out for liberation and human rights! The struggle for power and for oil and for weapons ruins the weak, enriches the wealthy, and gives power to the powerful. This divided world is increasingly capable of turning into a universal prison camp. And we are faced with the burning question: on which side of the barbed wire are we living, and at whose cost? The people in darkness see the great light. To this people – to them first of all – the light shines in all its brightness. To these people the child is born, for the peace of us all. Do we belong to this people, or do we cling to our own lights, our fortune-tellers and our own interpreters of the signs of the times, people who tell us what we want to hear, from Nostradamus and astrological calendars down to the learned interpreters of the laws of history?

The analysis of darkness and the denunciation of the crooked and the infamous can always arouse our interest, but they do not take us any further. The reasons for oppression and the powers behind it can easily be named, but that does not open the door to freedom for a single prisoner. Anyone who struggles in the night with the shadows of the night spreads shadows round himself. Anyone who fights in anarchy against anarchy easily becomes anarchistic. We have to cling to the light that disperses the shadows. There is no other way out of the darkness.

Why does the prophet talk here about the *light* shining in darkness? Is this just Christmas poetry? No. What he is proclaiming to the imprisoned people is quite simply God's new creation. Once again, and this time finally, it shines above the chaotic depths, as it shone over the world in the beginning when the earth was without form and void. Then it shone over the chaos of the waters. Now it is going to shine over the chaos of history. Now, as then, the light is the sign of the presence of God. Where the Lord, the creator of life, is present, inhuman oppression and bloody murder cease, and peace, justice and freedom spring to life. And the reverse is also true. Wherever this liberation comes about, whenever this jubilation is heard and armaments are banned, the creative God is present. His presence creates life that is lovely and peace that endures.

The real blackness of the darkness is the eclipse of God. So the true light in every enlightenment is the revelation of the creative God who makes the whole world dance. 'I am the light of the world; he who follows me will not walk in darkness, but will have the light of life,' says the revealer of God, according to John 8.12.

The prophet changes the image again. The word 'jubilation', just by itself, sounds like harvest festival, when everyone is filled according to his or her needs. Jubilation sounds from every joyous throat when the spoils are distributed and everyone receives his share. Jubilation without lament includes the harvest, but it is much more than harvest, the feast of nature, and it is far more than the division of the spoils, the feast of politics.

And then the prophet lays aside his images altogether and becomes realistic: God himself comes and lifts the yoke off the bowed shoulders of his people. He takes away the whips of the slave-drivers, breaking them over his knee, as it were, and throwing them into the fire. He tears down the power of the victors, the clashing iron shoes and the bloody coats, and throws them into the bonfire of his peace.

The Israelites long ago would have said that this was just what Gideon's little group experienced in the battle against the Midianites, when God alone was victorious. This, they must have said, was just what happened in the exodus of our fathers from slavery in Egypt. This was the way God conquered – just as alone, and just as surprisingly; and this is the way he will conquer at the end.

But more is promised here than can be expressed simply through old-soldier reminiscences. For God's victory does not come about through new armaments and force levied against force, or through alliances and solidarity. God has his own, divine kind of victory. For God's victory puts an end to all human wars and victories once and for all. It is a final victory, which serves peace, not one that leads to the next war, as our melancholy victories usually do. The prophet gives his images of war so alien an orientation that they actually describe the conquest of war. Every weapon becomes a flame, every aggression fuel for the fire. God's victory puts a final end to the victories of human beings. People lose their taste for them. Swords are turned into ploughshares and peace treaties replace the atom bombs.

But how is this supposed to happen? Does not the power to liberate the masses stem from rifles just as much as the forces of oppression? How can oppression and war be fought against and overcome without bringing new oppressions and new wars into the world, again with bloody coats and the tramp of boots through the streets?

All the images the prophet uses to paint the possible future point to one fact: the birth of the divine child. The burning of the weapons, the jubilation and the great light are all caught up in the birth of God's peace-bringer. They are all to be found in him. Now the prophet stops talking in intoxicating images and thrilling comparisons, and comes to the heart of the matter: the person of the divine liberator. 'To us a child is born. To us a son is given.' This future, that is to say, is wholly and entirely God's initiative. That is why it is so totally different from our human plans and possibilities. If liberation and peace are bound up with the birth of a little helpless and defenceless child, then their future lies in the hands of God alone. On the human side, all we can see here is weakness and helplessness. It is not the pride and strength of the grown man which are proclaimed on the threshold of the kingdom, but the defencelessness and the hope of the child.

The kingdom of peace comes through a child, and liberation is bestowed on the people who become as children: disarmingly defenceless, disarming through their defencelessness, and making others defenceless because they themselves are so disarming.

After the prophet's mighty visions of the destruction of all power and the forceful annihilation of all coercion, we are now suddenly face to face with this inconspicuous child. It sounds so paradoxical that some interpreters have assumed that this is a later interpolation. The prisoners who have to fight for their rights also find it difficult to understand how this child can help them. But it is really quite logical. For what the prophet says about the eternal peace of God which satisfies our longings can only come to meet us, whether we are frightened slaves or aggressive masters, in the form of the child. A child is defenceless. A child is innocent. A child is the beginning of a new life. His defencelessness makes our armaments superfluous. We can put away the rifles and open our clenched fists. His innocence redeems us from the curse of the evil act which is bound to breed ever more evil. We no longer have to go on like this. And his birth opens up for us the future of a life in peace that is different from all life hitherto, since that life was bound up with death.

'For to us a child is born. To us a son is given. The government is upon his shoulder.' The liberator becomes a pleading child in our world, armed to the teeth as it is. And this child will become the liberator for the new world of peace. That is why his rule means life, not death; peace, not war; freedom, not oppression. This sovereignty lies on the defenceless, innocent and hopeful shoulders of this child.

This makes our fresh start into the future meaningful and possible. The oppressed will be free from oppression. And they will also be free from the dreams of darkness, the visions of revenge. They stand up and rejoice, and their rejoicing frees their masters too from their brutal armaments. The oppressors with their cudgels, their iron shoes and their bloody coats will be freed from their grim machinations and will leave the poor in peace. For the new human being has been born, and a new humanity will be possible, a humanity which no longer knows either masters or slaves, either oppressed or oppressors. This is God's initiative on behalf of his betrayed and tormented humanity. 'The zeal of the Lord of hosts will do this.' It is the zeal of his ardent love.

There is no other initiative which we can seize with absolute assurance, for ourselves or for other people. There is no other zeal for the liberation of the world in which we can place a certain hope.

There are certainly many other movements, and much fervent zeal for the liberation of the masses. It certainly sounds more resolute for people in darkness to dream of God's day of vengeance, finding satisfaction in the hope that at the Last Judgment all the godless enemies who oppress us here will be cast into hell-fire. But what kind of blessedness is it which luxuriates in revenge and needs the groans of the damned as background to its own joy? To us a child is born, not an embittered old man. God in a child, not as hangman. That is why he prayed on his cross: 'Father, forgive them; for they know not what they do.' It sounded more heroic when, forty years ago, in 1934, the columns marched through Tübingen, singing with fanatical zeal: 'One day, the day of revenge. One day, and we shall be free.' It was a zeal that led to Auschwitz and Stalingrad.

For many people today it is perhaps more attractive to join in singing:

Then comrades, come rally,
and the last fight let us face.
The Internationale
Unites the human race.

But does that really lead one's brothers to the 'dawn that brings in a brighter day'? Does it not bring new shadows into the world?

I should not like there to be any misunderstanding at this point. It may be necessary, indeed unavoidable, to carry on the struggle against the marching feet by means of marching feet, and to break the rods of the slave-drivers with our own rods, provided that there is no doubt about the right to resistance. This right exists when laws are broken, constitutions are destroyed, or fundamental human rights are persistently infringed.

But even so, these struggles are still struggles in the night. They are not as yet the light of the final liberation. They are still caught up in the vicious circle of force and retaliation. They still do not bring lasting peace, or unswerving justice. The oppression of the poor is not a state of affairs with which one can rest content. The punishment of the oppressor is not a liberation over which one can rejoice.

The emperors have always liked to be called emperors of peace, from Augustus down to the present day. Their opponents and the heroes of the people have always liked to be called 'liberators', from Arminius of the Cherusci to Simón Bolívar. They have come and gone. Neither their rule nor their liberation endured. God was not with them. Their zeal was not the zeal of the Lord. They did not disarm this divided world. They could not forgive the guilt because they themselves were not innocent. Their hope did not bring new life. So let them go their way. Let us deny them our complete obedience. 'To us this child is born.' The divine liberty lies upon his shoulders.

What does his rule look like? We have to know this if we want to begin to live with him. He will establish 'peace on earth', we are told, and he will 'uphold peace with justice and with righteousness'. But how can peace go together with justice? What we are familiar with is generally peace based on injustice, and justice based on conflict. The life of justice is struggle. Among us, peace and justice are divided by the struggle for power. The so-called 'law of the strongest' destroys justice and right. The weakness of the peacemakers makes peace fragile. It is only in the zeal of love that what power has separated can be put together again: in a just peace and in the right to peace. This love does not mean accepting breaches of justice 'for the sake of peace', as we say. But it does not mean, either, breaking someone else's peace for the sake of our own rights. Peace and righteousness will only kiss and be one when the *new person* is born, and God the Lord, who has created all things, arrives at his just rights in his creation. When God is God in the world, then no one will want to be anyone else's Lord and God any more. Then no one will be able to be the servant and slave of anyone else. Then we shall literally leave one another in peace, give one another peace, because the very life of justice is the recognition of the other person in his human dignity.

But is this really possible here and now, or is it just a dream?

There is nothing against dreams if they are good ones. The prophet gave the people in darkness, and us, this unforgettable dream. We should remain true to it. But he could only see the shadowy outline of the name of the divine child, born for the freedom of the world; he called him wonderful counsellor, mighty hero, everlasting father, prince of peace.

The New Testament proclaims to us the person himself. He is Jesus Christ, the child in the manger, the preacher on the mount, the tormented man on the cross, the risen liberator.

So according to the New Testament the dream of a liberator, and the dream of peace, is not merely a dream. The liberator is already present and his power is already among us. We can follow him, even today making visible something of the peace, liberty and righteousness of the kingdom which he will complete. It is no longer impossible. It has become possible for us in fellowship with him. Let us share in his new creation of the world and – born again to a living hope – live as new men and women.

The zeal of the Lord be with us all.

Intercession

Lord, we do not pray for ourselves, but for your people who are sighing and suffering in darkness. We pray for the imprisoned, the deported, the exiled, the men and women who are reduced to silence in camps all over the world:

be with them in their necessity,
give them a steadfast heart
and bring them to freedom.
We pray for the sick, for handicapped children, for the dying and
for those among us who mourn:
be with them in their loneliness,
comfort them,
and give them a share in the fullness of your life.
We pray for those who have gone astray and for the embittered.
For all those who feel forsaken and whose lives have become empty
and meaningless, people who are unloved and have become
unloving:
in the zeal of your love, do not let them go;
give them a new spirit of assurance.
We name those we know in the silence of our hearts, as the
representatives of many; for we are their brothers and sisters.
Lord hear us and hear them.
Let your justice come and unjust power pass away.
Let your peace come and arms, war and retaliation pass away.
let your light come and the chaos in us and round about us pass
away.
But thanks be to God who gives us the victory through our Lord
Jesus Christ.

5 The New Covenant of Freedom

Behold, the days are coming, says the Lord, when I will make a new covenant with the house of Israel and the house of Judah, not like the covenant which I made with their fathers when I took them by the hand to bring them out of the land of Egypt; for they have broken my covenant and I have rejected them, says the Lord. But this is the covenant which I will make with the house of Israel after those days, says the Lord: I will put my law within them, and I will write it upon their hearts; and I will be their God, and they shall be my people.

And no longer shall each man teach his neighbour and each his brother, saying, 'Know the Lord,' for they shall all know me, from the least of them to the greatest, says the Lord; for I will forgive their iniquity, and I will remember their sin no more (Jer. 31.31–34).

Sermons will be superfluous. No one will have to preach them and no one will have to listen to them. Church will be superfluous. No one will have to attend services or pay their financial dues. Clergy, teachers, professors and students of theology will be superfluous. The theological faculties can be closed down. The teaching ministry of the church will be superfluous, whether it is fallible or infallible, in Rome, Tübingen, or wherever it may be. The Bible, both the Old and the New Testaments, the interpretation of Scripture and the disputes about the Bible will all be superfluous. It is all superfluous, and it all comes to an end, once it has achieved its purpose, when – yes, when 'the days come' in which God will make the new, final, indestructible covenant with men and women. When God will write his law *in their hearts*; when God will be our God in our inmost being; when we become his people with all our hearts, then, 'No one will teach and preach to the other any longer, saying "Know the Lord", for they shall all know him, face to face, from the greatest of them to the least.'

But can we ever free ourselves from those great authorities, the Bible, the church, religion? We have to lean on something. We incline – incline far too much – to cling to authority, even if we are occasionally overtaken by a fit of anti-authoritarianism. Authorities relieve us of difficult decisions. They release us from the weight of responsibility. But the more they relieve us, the more they estrange us too. The more they make our decisions for us, the more they cheat us of the happiness of our full, independent responsibility. Anyone who always lets himself be rocked in the cradle of security will never stand on his own feet. Anyone who always wants to be kept safe never learns to walk upright. Anyone who always lets himself be guided and led will never raise his head and become a person in his own right.

God wants people who have come of age, people who make their own decisions and take responsibility for what they do. God wants free people, who stand on their own feet and are themselves. God doesn't want copies; he wants originals.

This means that every sermon lives from the awareness that it is superfluous. Once it has evoked faith, it comes to an end. Every church is an interim, a provisional measure, scaffolding. When the kingdom of God comes, the scaffolding will be abolished. Every true theology knows that it is fragmentary: the person who looks on God with a pure heart no longer needs concepts about him.

But it is only when this new covenant has become reality that the church will be superfluous, not before. Up to then it is still necessary. Every sermon is a promise. The Bible, the church and theology are all fragments of hope. It is only when this hope has been fulfilled that the fragments can be forgotten, not before. Until then they are necessary. The Bible, the church, preaching and theology will only come to an end when they have arrived at their goal. But what is that goal?

For the prophet, the goal is *the new covenant*. What is a covenant? What is the purpose of a covenant with God? What did the old covenant consist of, and what was bad about it? What is the new covenant supposed to be, and what is good about that?

What Jeremiah here calls 'the old covenant' is nothing less than Israel's experience of its roots, the heart of the Jewish faith, which is celebrated year by year in the Passover. It is Israel's exodus from slavery in Egypt into the liberty of the promised land. It is *the covenant of freedom*, made on Sinai, defined and preserved in the Ten Commandments. 'The God of Abraham, Isaac and Jacob' is not the divine Lord of the Pharaohs, the Caesars and the slave-owners. He is the Father of the humiliated, the saviour of the oppressed. He led his people out of slavery into the liberty of the promised land. He does not want slaves or vassals. He wants the free comrades and friends of his covenant. He leads his people out of their infancy into the full responsibility of their own history. 'I am the Lord your God who brought you out of the house of bondage.' That is who he is, he himself, himself wholly and totally. And this is also the first commandment of our liberty: 'You shall have no other gods beside me.' For you need no other gods beside me.

The exodus has an external, political side: the liberation of the oppressed. It also has an inward, spiritual side: the imposition of free life in the covenant with this God and with him alone. The people who celebrate this fundamental experience every Passover can only praise God and their own liberty in a single breath. Of this people it can truly be said that 'whoever loves God loves freedom'. Anyone who is afraid of freedom is afraid of God. Anyone who suppresses freedom suppresses God.

Liberation movements, old and new, religious and political, have continually come back to this experience of Israel's, this experience of 'God and freedom'. The exodus theme has run through all the European reformations and revolutions. It has filled the oppressed and the humiliated with the spirit of God, which is the spirit of liberty. And this will be so in the future too. I believe that some people will have doubts here because in the future the liberation is not going to be ours; it will be other people who want to liberate themselves – have to liberate themselves – from *us*.

But what is wrong with this covenant which followed the 'political' exodus? What can be greater than external and internal liberation, or go beyond it?

The old covenant could be broken. It could be broken, not because

God was unreliable, but because human beings, as they are, are unstable beings. Anyone who relies on people is all too often left in the lurch. This was God's experience in the covenant he made with his human beings. It could be broken by people – and by the very same people who had been liberated. They misused the liberty they had been given, because they could evidently not endure it. 'They have broken my covenant and I have cast them aside', was the divine judgment Jeremiah heard.

Why did they break the covenant? Was God's mighty act in history when he liberated them from Egyptian bondage not convincing enough after all? Was the covenant, with the Ten Commandments, too demanding? Had the Lord overestimated the people he had chosen? Everything had apparently been done from God's side which was necessary for the covenant of freedom: the saving act had proved God to be the dependable and mighty One. The covenant, with the Ten Commandments, was not an unduly severe obligation for the liberated people.

And yet something is evidently lacking. God reveals himself in the historical liberation of the people; God reveals his will in the tables of the law – and the people remain inwardly just the same as before: vacillating, unstable, obstinate, incorrigible. They have experienced everything necessary for the salvation of freedom. They have only failed to change *themselves*. They *themselves* have not become free. 'Change conditions, and people will change', some left-wing revolutionaries believe, and in recent times some right-wing ones too. But people are not so obliging. They will not even do it for God's sake. God changed all the conditions for his people of Israel, but they *themselves*, their hearts, were not the hearts of independent, responsible people. The external liberation was too much for them. They were not up to it, as we say. That is why the blessing given to faithfulness was replaced by God's curse, which is given to faithlessness. The person who abandons God is himself abandoned by God.

But if God has to respond to the breach of loyalty by rejecting the people, what happens to their election? Did not the promise, 'I will be your God and you shall be my people', precede the covenant and the Ten Commandments? Is not this assurance of God's absolute, for God's sake? 'God is faithful. He cannot deny himself,' the New Testament tells us. That is why the prophet Jeremiah looks beyond the catastrophe into which the faithless people are being drawn because of their rejection of their God. He does not speculate about a possible future. Instead he looks into God's heart. He senses God's irrevocable passion for men and women. And so he sees 'the days' coming in which this God will remain faithful to himself and his resolve, in spite of all his justifiable anger over his wretched people. And for that reason the new covenant will come, as surely as God is God.

The new covenant is not totally new. It is rather a reconstruction of the truth of the old covenant: 'I will be their God and they shall be my people.' That was the content of the old covenant, and it is the subject of the new one too. But this fellowship with God is now to be unbreakable and indestructible. That is what is behind the promise, 'I will write my law in their hearts.' This means that there is no longer any difference between the commandment and the deed, between duty and inclination. Everyone knows the will of God *in* his heart, and *by* heart. He performs it of his own accord, without compulsion, without any threats, without the prospect of any reward. Doing good is no longer a task or a duty. It is a delight and a matter of course. A person does what is good just because it is good, not because it has been commanded, not out of fear, and not out of hope. The law is no longer law for anyone for whom God's law is 'written in the heart'. He has become a new person. He no longer lives 'under' the law, threatened and impelled by it. He lives 'in' the law. He is righteous. 'Love and do what you like', as Augustine rightly put it.

The new covenant knows a divine liberation of which the exodus covenant knew nothing. God does not merely liberate people from slavery and political tyranny. He also frees them from the imprisonment of sin and from the torments of guilt. 'I will forgive their iniquity, and I will remember their sin no more.' That is the inward liberation which has to be added to the outward one, if people are to be led into freedom truly and completely.

God liberates people from tyranny and childish dependence; that is the first thing. God liberates people from guilt and sin; that is the second thing. The two belong together. No one can aim at the one without the other, unless he is prepared to remain a slave. Liberation without reconciliation easily leads to the subjection of reality to terrorist pressures. But reconciliation without liberation easily putrifies into delaying tactics, a mere exhortation to patience.

But does this 'new covenant' really exist? Have 'the days' which Jeremiah already talked about 2,500 years ago actually dawned? Or is this still a dream – a beautiful dream but, when all is said and done, a mere utopia and not even a particularly practical utopia at that, if we look at the ugly inhumanity of human beings?

And another question is more important still. To whom does the new covenant apply? Who is going to have the law written in his heart? Who is going to know God in his inmost self like this? According to Jeremiah, the covenant is going to be made with Israel, not with us Gentiles. So what has it to do with us? What right do we really have to appropriate Israel's hopes for ourselves?

It is true that we are Gentiles, not Israelites. But through the Jew Jesus Christ we have access to Israel's hopes for 'the new covenant'. Why? Because through Jesus the liberating act of 'the new covenant' has come to the Gentiles. 'I will forgive their iniquity, and I will remember their sin no more.' This is 'the new covenant in my blood, shed for many', for Jews and Gentiles, and for every one of us. Through Jesus, God's boundless mercy has become manifest. Through him we Gentiles discover that God does not punish guilt but pardons it; that he does not hold our sins against us but forgives them. And so Israel's hopes have become our hopes too.

Does this then mean that in Christ the new covenant has already come into being? Yes, we Christians would like to think so. But it is not the case. For if it had already been fulfilled in Christ there would be no more sermons, no more church and no more theology. Then we should all, 'from the least of us to the greatest', know God as he is. But this is not yet so, in the church either. And yet the first of these wonderful hopes has already become an actual experience: the forgiveness of guilt, the forgiveness of sins. And the other one has also become a reality and not mere utopia: the experience of the divine Spirit in our hearts. That is not yet the whole of 'the new covenant'. But it is the beginning of 'the days' which the prophet promised.

With the forgiveness of guilt the new covenant – the new beginning – starts. This new covenant consists of direct knowledge of God, and the law written in the heart. What does this mean?

In this life direct knowledge of God is the experience of faith, experience of the self in faith, the experience of God in one's own self. Certainly, there is also the childish belief in authority: I believe in God because my parents told me to, because the church tells me to, because the Bible tells me to. But faith like this is only knowledge at second hand. We are believing what other people claim to have experienced. We are holding to be true what other people think they have seen to be the truth. The Enlightenment, especially Lessing and Kant, rightly saw that this kind of faith is not yet faith in the true sense. 'Prophecies which I myself experience as having been fulfilled are one thing; prophecies of which I merely know historically that others claim to have experienced their fulfilment are another. Miracles that I see with my own eyes are one thing; miracles of which I merely know historically that others claim to have seen them are another.'

'I myself' – that is the point at issue here. That is the point at issue in true faith. I, I myself, am loved by God. I, I myself step outside my social role, with all the duties and tasks its institutions impose on me, and stand there all by myself, as it were, recognizing God in me and myself in God. Nothing and no one stands between him and me any more. He is there – and I am there. The more certain I am of myself, the more certain I am of his nearness. Anyone who begins to sense this can no longer lose himself. He will no longer yield up his life to external authorities. He will begin to live himself. He has become an independent person. He looks on God with his heart and lives every moment 'before his face'.

Anyone who in faith experiences himself and God, God and himself, gains courage and confidence in himself. He believes because he has *himself* seen the truth and become convinced of it. He no longer needs any external authorities for this, neither the church nor the Bible. He acknowledges the truth because it is God's truth, not because it is in the Bible or because the church teaches it. This is the Christian come of age.

Are preaching, the church and theology then all superfluous for this person? No, they are not superfluous; but they have become transitions – bridges, roads, vehicles, media. The childish faith in authority strives to become independent faith. Then it has achieved its goal. The historical faith of the church wants to become the personal faith of reason and the heart. Then it has achieved its goal. And the faith of the Bible has to lead to the evidence of the Spirit and of power. Then its witness has been fulfilled. I perceive the truth myself. I believe, because it is my own experience. I myself find God in myself and myself in God. I have become God's friend. That is the new covenant in faith.

The law written in the heart: for this we use the word 'conscience'. In the new covenant the experience of one's own conscience takes the place of the tables of the law. I experience the divine will in the bad conscience that accuses me. I experience it in the good conscience that justifies and mobilizes me. By 'making a conscience', as we say, out of one thing or another, I begin to take over responsibility for my personal life and for life in society. If I decide according to my own conscience, then I and I alone have to take the consequences, with God and before God. I can no longer hide behind force of circumstances, or deference for others, or duty.

In the experience of the conscience, and in decisions of conscience, every one of us is just himself, a person before God and himself. No ecclesiastical magisterium or teaching ministry can intervene on our behalf, to take the weight off our conscience, whether it be contraception or conscientious objection that is in question.

No one relieves us of our own responsibility. The person who would like to do so wants to rob us of our liberty, and hence of our conscience, and hence too of the new covenant. There is no doubt that sole responsibility to conscience is a principle that has also been misused. Some people have therefore preferred to impose an 'imperative mandate' on the people who represent them. But if there is a force which makes people able and ready, if necessary, to become 'strangers to their own people' and to oppose mass madness and mass seduction, then it is the conscience. It is the conscience which gives people the strength to obey God rather than human beings. It is conscience which makes a person prepared to be lonely rather than without backbone, and to die rather than let his own identity be broken. It is the experience of conscience, and God in the conscience, which strengthens one's resolution when other people begin to truckle to authority, or go along with the crowd. Anyone who experiences God in his conscience has come of age as a person.

Does this make the church, theology and ethics superfluous? No, but they become transitions. No teaching ministry and no official statement made by church dignataries can relieve our consciences of their own decisions. For no church can relieve us of our responsibility before God. The church's teaching ministry can advise the conscience, but it cannot bind it. The commandments, and the interpretation of the commandments by other Christians, can school our consciences, but can never, ever, relieve us of our own decisions.

I have to do what is good for its own sake. I can do what is just because it is just. I must take responsibility for what is evil; and the deed left undone weighs on *my* conscience, not on the conscience of the church. I myself recognize what is good. I myself do it – or leave it undone. God takes me seriously as a person. That is the new covenant in the conscience. The law is written in our hearts. So let us discern this law in our hearts, and our hearts in the law.

Finally: we shall all know God, 'from the least to the greatest'. No one is too great, no one is too small. No one has to look up to anyone. No one has to look down on anyone. Great or small, man or woman, black or white, handicapped or non-handicapped – where God is known, the differences disappear and the democracy of the Holy Spirit begins.

6 The Blessedness of the Peacemakers

Blessed are the peacemakers, for they shall be called children of God (Matt. 5.9).

Prayer
Heavenly Father,
it is time for you to come,
for our time is running out
and our world is passing away.
You gave us life, one with another,
and we have destroyed it in conflict.
You made your creation in harmony and balance.
We want progress, and are perishing through our strivings for
    it.
Come, Creator of all things,
and renew the face of the earth.
In our unhappiness give us hope for your day,
the day when we can laugh in peace with all created beings,
and praise you to all eternity.

Lord Jesus Christ,
our brother on our way.
Give peace to our enemies.
Take from us our fear of death.
Make us ready to walk beside you
and to love our enemies.
We hope for your kingdom
as we hope for peace.
Come, Lord Jesus, come soon.

Holy Spirit,
we know you as power from on high
and as consolation in the depths.
We cry to you,
and you respond within us.
We fall silent,
and you speak for us with your yearning.
Come, Creator Spirit,
give us dreams of peace
and visions of freedom.
Make us inconsolable when they are betrayed.
Console us when they are disappointed.

God, Father, Son and Holy Spirit, triune God:
unite with yourself your torn and divided world,
and let us all be one in you,
for it is in you that we all live and move and have our being.

When we are face to face with the Sermon on the Mount, it is
impossible to remain general and uncommitted. It cuts into our lives
and makes a decision inescapable. The question facing us today is:
'Do we keep up with the arms race or live without armaments?' It is
a question of life and death. Whatever answer we give, the survival
of mankind, or the death of every living thing on earth, depends on
our decision. The curtain has gone up on the final act.

But who is certain that his answer will serve life and not death?
Because of this, many people find the answer so difficult that they
would like to suppress the challenge of the question, and refuse to
accept it at all. It is really a matter of conscience. We shall have to
bear the responsibility for our answer, whether it is to arm or to have
the will and purpose to live without armaments. But who can really
bear the responsibility for his answer? Which of us will not one day
stand there in consternation and say, 'But that wasn't what I
intended'?

Let us, this morning, first try to clear our minds about the real
situation, so that we can discern the seriousness and the inescapability
of the question. Having done this, we will confront our answers with
the divine love of our enemies that is offered to us, as we have just
heard in Jesus' Sermon on the Mount.

Peace is God's first word and his last, for he himself is the fullness and the riches of peace, and its indestructible fortress. That is why the Memorandum issued by the German Protestant Churches in 1969 stated: 'God desires to live with human beings in a kingdom of peace.' Because of this, the whole Christian church is quite unequivocally bound to the service of peace. But what does peace mean here?

Peace is not merely the absence of war; it is also the overcoming of injustice and oppression. In positive terms, it is life that is blessed, affirmed, loved and successful – life as *shalom*. Anyone who wants to serve peace must serve life. He must therefore resist war, because this is the deadliest form of discord. But this resistance against war is only one part of a much wider devotion to life. The service of peace is the whole task of life. And the prevention of murder, homicide and war is only one part of this life-work.

There always have been, and still are, two attitudes to war among Christians. Some people reject, completely and fundamentally, every act of violence, even acts of violence which are supposed to hinder other acts of the same kind. Another group supports the rearmament of one's own nation where this is designed to prevent acts of war by means of the threat of violence. These two attitudes are reflected today in the alternative: are we going to live without armaments, and therefore without defence? Or are we going to 'secure peace' through armaments and by keeping up with the arms race?

Anyone who is not a pacifist always develops a doctrine about 'the just war'. This does not mean justifying war in itself; it means that war has to be subjected to the standards of justice. Is this still possible today? We are caught up in the arms systems of West or East, both of which are in a position to destroy all higher forms of life on earth many times over, by the methods of mass destruction – nuclear, chemical and bacterial. So we have to ask ourselves whether there can be such a thing as a 'just nuclear war' today. Some people have replied that indiscriminate mass destruction can never be justified, and that the strategy of 'massive retaliation' is unjustifiable; but that it is still possible to justify the limited use of nuclear weapons against military targets. The further development of nuclear weapons has evidently been adapted to this morality; neutron bombs and cruise missiles can be directed against specific military targets without destroying the whole population. This is the strategy of the limited nuclear war. Weapons have become more easily usable and applicable. The threshold of their application has therefore been considerably lowered. So this development towards the 'limited nuclear war' has not made peace any more secure; it has made it much less so.

The next justification of armaments is the doctrine of 'just nuclear rearmament', in order to gain time for disarmament and for a peace free of threats. Mutual intimidation prevents nuclear war and gains time – an interval, a period of grace for peace negotiations. This was, and is, the view held by most Christians in Germany. For these people, it is right to possess nuclear weapons, and to employ them as a threat; but it is not right to use them. Their possession can be a lever to gain time for a peace without any such weapons. But this view is based on more than one amiable delusion. In the first place, if a country is not prepared to use what it possesses, possession is no deterrent. Secondly, once one possesses these weapons, they have continually to be modernized, and one must continually 'catch up' if one's opponent seems to have 'got ahead'. This means that there is never an equilibrium in armaments; there is merely a parallel arms race. In the wake of a continual rearmament-spiral it is hard to arrive at a spiral of disarmament. Thirdly, the whole of society today is being imperceptibly orientated towards rearmament, so that we are gradually arriving at a comprehensive mobilization. We are getting used to it. We are getting used to what is totally unusual. We are being drawn into the whirlpool and cannot escape from it. Today the pressures of all these circumstances have taken on apocalyptic dimensions. Is the method madness? Is the madness becoming method? Can we still turn back at all? Is the system of deterrents in which we live still open to re-examination? Or is this the final act, the beginning of the end? And who can take the responsibility if this is so?

Twenty years ago, many people began to believe that a peace policy was possible, and that we could turn aside from this deadly development. As a result, the 'Ban the Bomb' movement died a natural death. Today many people are evidently again losing hope and are despairing of a new beginning. They say that the arms race is leading inescapably to universal death. It is already draining the life-blood of the nations, and using up all the resources with which we could overcome world-wide famine. For these people the question is: do we go along, or do we opt out? Rearming for the sake of disarming is no longer possible. So we have to follow the men who sired the bomb. When Einstein, Oppenheimer and the Russian Zacharov began to see where developments were leading – developments to which they themselves had made so essential a contribution – they opted out.

'Living without armaments' can have two different dimensions. There are Christians who put the discipleship of Christ above their responsibility for the world and renounce every act of violence, even acts of violence designed to hinder violence itself. But they do not make their personal decision the yardstick for general political action for other Christians and non-Christians. They know that a faith of this kind is not for everyone. This was the course chosen by the Anabaptists in the Reformation period: they held that the perfection of Christ could not be lived within the order of the sword. They chose defencelessness, peaceableness, preparedness for suffering, and death. The Anabaptist preacher Michael Sattler was cruelly put to death for his testimony to peace in 1528, in Rottenburg am Neckar. Secondly, Christians and non-Christians are opting out of the arms race and are turning their readiness to live without armaments into the political axiom of disarmament through first, unilateral concessions: 'Abolish nuclear weapons – in the Netherlands first of all.'

If we make the first choice, the risk is a personal one. If we make the second, it is a social one, too. In the first case a person takes the fatal consequences of his actions on himself. In the second case he also requires them of his family, his children and his nation.

So anyone who is prepared to live without armaments must, if it comes to the point, also be prepared to die without armaments, to look on at oppression without resistance, and to surrender his country to a quite conceivable Gulag Archepelago. But who can take the responsibility for this? Rearm, or live without armaments? I hope I have presented the two decisions objectively, along with the reasons for them and their dangers. But up to now both sides have built up their case as if there were neither God nor Christ, nor the Sermon on the Mount, whose challenge we have just heard. Yet this introduces a factor into the calculation which brings us up short and changes everything. This factor is *the reality of God*, which is in fact the reality that sustains us all.

'You are the children of your Father in heaven.' This reminder calls us out of the conflict. Anyone who allows himself to be drawn into conflict, or carries on a conflict, is subject to the law of retaliation.

There is no other way of preserving an equilibrium in the struggle: an eye for an eye, a tooth for a tooth – arm, rearm – rearm, arm. But anyone who becomes involved in the law of retaliation towards his enemy is drawn into a vicious circle from which he can never escape. He will become his enemy's enemy, and a terror to the one who terrifies him. He threatens what threatens him, and hates what hates him. He increasingly takes his colouring from his enemy. If evil is requited by evil, then the one evil takes its bearings from the other, and that is fatal. We are only liberated from vicious circles like this if we cease to take our bearings from our enemy, and when another person is more important to us.

'You are the children of your Father in heaven.' That is *the new orientation*. It may sound like a childlike assurance of harmony and safe-keeping. But here we have to take it quite literally. If you are your heavenly Father's children, then free yourselves from enmity, and take your bearings from the Father alone! Do not debase yourselves any longer! Do not lose yourselves in enmity! You are intended for something different, and another is looking after you.

If we want to know what it means to be 'a child of God', we have to look at Jesus, the Son. He called God his Father and became the friend of the enemies of his class and his nation, a friend of sinners and tax-collectors. He called God his Father and went to his death without defending himself, praying for his murderers as he died. The disciples who followed him were therefore right to call him 'Son of God', for he was no one else's son and belonged to no other party.

In community with that Son of God from Nazareth we discover who God the Father is, and find out what it means to be his child on earth. We have been the enemies of our enemies long enough. In the discipleship of Jesus we experience the liberating power of love, love that is quite literally disarming.

The love which Jesus put in the place of retaliation is love of our enemy. Mutual love is nothing special. It only means repaying good with good. But love of our enemy is not love as repayment; it is prevenient and creative love. Anyone who repays evil with good is truly free. He no longer merely reacts. He creates something new. He follows nothing but his own resolve, and no longer lets the rules of action be dictated by his opponent. Jesus did not die cursing his enemies, but with a prayer for them on his lips. He gave his life for the people who condemned him and put him to death. In his life, his sufferings and his death, he revealed to us the perfection of God. 'Be perfect as your heavenly Father is perfect.'

But in what does God's perfection consist? Certainly not in perfectionism in any sense. It lies in the love which is long-suffering, patient and kind, which bears no grudge, which endures all things, believes all things, hopes all things (I Cor. 13). God loves his enemies, blesses them, does good to them, and does not set evil against evil: that is his perfection. And it is from this that we all live. From this the whole world lives, even if it does not know it. God sustains and preserves everything, because he has hope for everyone. His perfection is his limitless capacity for suffering. He is all-powerful because he is all-enduring. His uniqueness is the unfathomably creative power of his love.

If this were not so, none of us would be able to talk about the love of God he or she has experienced; for he loved us when we were still his enemies. While we were godless, Christ died for us. And his Spirit disarms us when we want to be the enemies of other people. God's children – that means the enemies whom God has overcome. They are disarmed. They become creative. They can no longer repay evil with evil. They must always discover some way of doing good in return for the evil done to them We escape from the vicious circle of mutual deterrents and follow another law, the law of the creative God. We see the sun of a new day. It dawns on the evil and the good, making no distinction between them. God gives life and the warmth of life to all of us – to the evil first of all, because they need it most. We feel the rain which falls on the parched earth and makes it fruitful. In the same way God lets the rain fall on the just and the unjust, so that they too may live – here first of all on the just, because they need it. These are the great images for the new orientation towards God which liberates us.

And there is something else behind this image too: the sun is there for everyone, the rain is there for everyone. 'Love your enemies, do good to those who hate you, pray for those who persecute you.' When this happens, the sun rises over the gloomy valley, and the rain falls on the parched ground. Love of our enemies is the sunrise of life, and the realistic condition for the survival of humanity.

Keep up with the arms race or live without armaments? Up to now we have only asked: what is in the interests of our security, what is in the interests of our survival? But the question is now: what is in the interests of our enemy, and what helps him most? How can we best bless those who curse us? How can we do good to those who hate us? Let us be practical about this. We Germans are afraid of the Russians and of almost nothing else. So we have to ask ourselves: what will help the Russian people most to find freedom in peace – our rearmament, or our disarmament? How can we bless the Communists who curse us? How can we do good to the peoples in the 'Third World', who think we are their enemies?

Our security policy is, after all, largely a policy of fear. And a policy of fear is a policy of self-seeking. Creative love, on the other hand, love of our enemies, only springs from freedom – from the glorious liberty of being a child of the eternal God, and from freedom from the fear of a temporal death.

Can we really be *free* of this fear? We will be more completely free of it if we recognize the danger, and deliberately accept the risk. Our freedom and serenity will be in proportion to our awareness of the risk of a vulnerable, defenceless but creative life. It is only the unknown and what we have suppressed that fills us with anxiety.

Martin Luther King pointed out when he was in prison in Alabama that non-violent resistance against evil was not a method for cowards, but was the way of the strong. The soul of the white man had suffered, and it was only through the love of his black brothers that he could overcome his inhibitions, his insecurity and his anxieties. Because this inner liberty has to be discovered anew every day, the first commandment of the Christian civil rights movement of 1963 was to 'meditate daily on the teachings and life of Jesus'. To this we can add nothing except 'Amen'.

7 Revolutionary Love of our Enemies

You have heard that it was said, 'You shall love your neighbour and hate your enemy.' But I say to you, Love your enemies and pray for those who insult and persecute you, so that you may be children of your Father who is in heaven; for he makes his sun rise on the evil and on the good, and sends rain on the just and on the unjust. For if you love those who love you, what reward have you? Do not even the tax collectors do the same? And if you salute only your brethren, what more are you doing than others? Do not even the Gentiles do the same? You, therefore, must be perfect, as your heavenly Father is perfect (Matt. 5.43–48).

Prayer
Heavenly Father,
we call upon you in Jesus' name. We come with empty hands. We have not been able to love our enemies. As a rule we have never even seen them. We have avoided them. When we saw them, we felt only fear and anger, not love.

So we come to you, not as the children of your love, but as the enemy of our enemies, beseeching you for ourselves and all the others:

bless those who curse you, do good to those who hate you. Forgive us for what we have failed to do for our enemies.

You lead us out of the constriction of fear and out of the prison of hate, into the wide space of freedom. Let us see your sun, which rises upon the evil and the good, and rejoice in its warmth, together with our enemies.

Here for the first time in the Sermon on the Mount, we have the word
which is the common denominator for everything else: *love*. And it
is used from the outset quite uncompromisingly and in an unambigu-
ous definition: *love of one's enemy*. All other love is a matter of
course. Te repay like by like, both in the good sense and the bad, is
nothing out of the way. It is normal. But love of one's enemy is
special, extraordinary. It is something that is specifically Christian,
the 'more', the 'better righteousness'. It is from this that we are
supposed to be able to recognize the men and women who are free,
God's children.

Yet humanly speaking, love of one's enemy is impossible, 'contrary
to nature': the leopard cannot change his spots, as we say. So love of
our enemies is the thing that is different, the thing that is divine. 'He
makes his sun rise on the evil – on the evil first of all – and on the
good.' Love of our enemies is the secret of Jesus that corresponds to
God himself. Jesus blessed the people who cursed him. He prayed for
the people who tortured him. He did not retaliate, but took suffering
upon himself for love's sake. He died for his enemies on the cross.
And so he died for us.

If it has not been clear before, it becomes evident at this point that
the whole Sermon on the Mount is nothing without the preacher,
and the path he took to that other mountain: Golgotha. In his
fellowship and in his discipleship the impossible becomes possible.
People love where they have hated; they bless where they have cursed;
evil is repaid by good. The secret of the Sermon on the Mount is not
its high moral ideals. It is Jesus himself. Once we understand him, we
understand his demands. If we do not understand him, the demands
remain alien, scandalous or simply foolish.

By telling us to love our enemies, the man from Nazareth as it were
treads firmly on all our toes at once. For loving our enemies
presupposes that we have them. Do we really have enemies? Do we
not prefer to avoid anything so unpleasant? So what enemies does
Jesus expect us to have? But if we really do have enemies, surely love
is impossible? Have we not to fight it out and see it through? Can we
throw ourselves to our enemies as we throw a bone to a dog? To have
enemies and to love them – both demands are strange. They make us
feel uneasy.

Let us look at the first of these requirements. Love of our enemies evidently presupposes the existence of enemies. We do not like this. In our prosperous bourgeois 'Christian' society, we are afraid of open enmity. We prefer to avoid conflicts. It is not merely in politics that we have discovered the famous method of 'leaving knotty problems on one side'. Contradictions are glossed over. Disputed points are simply struck off the agenda. Unsolved problems are repressed, shelved, or packed in cotton wool and pushed off on to the next generation. Instead of enemies and love of our enemies, we have chosen the tepid world of 'Be nice to one another'. Love, peace, cheerfulness; or moderation, sweet reasonableness, forbearance; or conformity, concessions and tolerance: these are our methods of simultaneously avoiding the scandal of having an enemy and the difficulty of loving him. After all, we have to get on with everyone somehow, whether they are pleasant or unpleasant, if we are to get along at all ourselves. We have become more or less unassailable, because we no longer take anything really seriously. We do not willingly attack anyone, either in anger or in love, because we no longer take anyone seriously. 'Live and let live.' So we get along splendidly – or do we?

I am sorry to say that, when I look at the Jesus of the Sermon on the Mount, I find him a trouble-maker, a spoil-sport who interferes with our party games. It was not Jesus who said 'Be nice to one another'. What he said was: 'I have not come to bring peace but a sword', and 'he who does not take up his cross and follow me is not worthy of me' (Matt. 10.34,38). Enmity is bound to arise for truth's sake. Jesus suffered from this enmity himself. By going to the people who were hated and despised, he made their enemies his own. By bringing the law-breakers and the lawless God's prevenient and undivided love, he drew upon himself the enmity of the law and its guardians. As we know, he was persecuted, hated, mocked, and finally cast out and crucified outside the gate. His disciples, who left everything and followed him, also experienced the enmity of their relations, friends, and the members of their own nation and religion. Jesus promised his friends nothing different. True peace with God in the community of his people brings discontent with the world of lies. True reconciliation with God evokes conflict with an unreconciled society. Anyone who is 'a child of his Father in heaven' – and how innocent that sounds! – becomes a trouble-maker and a spoil-sport in a world which has settled down without God, with the law of retaliation. 'Niceness' is lost to the person who chooses the way of Jesus. He *is* no one's enemy, but he *acquires* enemies. That is unavoidable. The Preacher on the Mount supposes us to have enemies because it is to our enemies that we are supposed to do good.

And then comes the second point. If we have enemies for the sake of truth and righteousness, then it is surely expecting even more of us to demand that we love those enemies. The Old Testament already tells us: 'If your enemy is hungry, give him bread to eat; and if he is thirsty, give him water to drink' (Prov. 25.21). And in quite practical terms: 'If you meet your enemy's ox or his ass going astray, you shall bring it back to him' (Ex. 23.4). This is what people were told even in those days. Nothing was said about simply hating one's enemies. So anyone who believes that the Communists are his enemies, and God's, ought to feed them when they are hungry. For example, we should send food and medical supplies to *all* Vietnam. Anyone who thinks that the capitalists are his enemies, and the enemies of his class, should not slaughter their oxen or interfere with their asses. Now at this point, if not before, one is bound to hear outraged voices raised in objection. 'No country can be ruled by way of the Sermon on the Mount,' Bismarck said, thereby showing himself to be 'a practical politician.'. 'It is impossible to stage a revolt by means of the Sermon on the Mount,' declared Herbert Marcuse in 1968 in Berlin, thereby proving himself to be 'a practical revolutionary'. A student had asked him: 'Does not hate of the imperialists lead to loss of humanity, so that for the revolutionary the enemy ceases to be human at all?' And Marcuse answered: 'The hate of exploitation and repression is *a humane element. . .* Nothing is more appalling than that exhortation of love "do not hate your enemy" in a world in which hate has been completely institutionalized.' He did, however, add: 'One can strike an opponent and defeat him without cutting off his ears or his legs, and without torturing him.'

But anyone who gives way to hate and retaliation towards his enemies is drawn into a vicious circle from which neither he nor the other person can escape unscathed. Hate eats into a person, if he has nothing with which to counter it. The Old Testament law, '*one* eye for an eye, *one* tooth for a tooth', is relatively humane compared with the deadly spiral we see everywhere, as violence escalates and hate outbids hate. First of all the enemy is de-humanized: he becomes the sub-human 'red', or the yellow rat, or the black nigger. He turns into the terrorist who has to be eradicated, or the devilish capitalist who has to be trodden under foot. Hate turns the enemy into a devil and kills him with words and pictures. This makes it easier to shoot him or liquidate him later on. But anyone who becomes his enemy's enemy begins to take on the reflection of his opponent's picture of him. When two people enter into the clinch of hate and begin to exchange blows and reprisals, they become more and more alike. Accentuated hate then makes the enemy responsible for everything we are prepared to do to him. In this way the images of our enemy conjured up by our aggression are generally highly significant self-portraits. If evil is repaid by evil, the one evil always conforms to the other. In the vicious circle of retaliation, one person becomes the other person's devil. Whether we put it in religious terms and say 'I hate those, Lord, who hate thee', and are glad when the godless murder one another (or at least get into economic difficulties); or whether we express the same idea in secular or ideological terms – in either case hate distorts the features, roughens the voice, and destroys the remains of humanity, making any humane purpose unconvincing.

Without the Sermon on the Mount there is neither any humane government, nor any humane revolt against injustice and exploitation. Without the crucified Preacher on the Mount, and people who follow *him*, instead of their enemies, the lights will go out, and this world will perish in the vicious circle of mutual retribution. The morgue of history proves it. And on the day when we remember the dead of two world wars, we should be aware of the fact.

Enmity for truth's sake is inescapable. But then how, in the midst of this hostility, can love of our enemy be possible? Surely only if we cease to ask what the enemy has done to us and the people we love, and ask solely *what Jesus did*. In the vicious circle of enmity, we all become vicious ourselves. My opponent puts his impress on me, and forces the conflict on me. Anyone who gazes only at the enemy becomes an enemy himself. It is only when something else is more important, only when another liberates me from this vicious circle, that this orientation towards the enemy stops, and a new game begins.

So who are we? Who puts their stamp on us? The Preacher on the Mount says: Be children of your Father who is in heaven. So love your enemies. Be perfect as your Father in heaven is perfect. *This* is what we are now meant to be. This is the new liberation. To be a child of God – oh yes, who wouldn't like to be that? It sounds like childlike security and harmony – Christmas everywhere. But with Jesus it does not look like that. He called God 'my Father', and left his family, his friends, and his secure existence for a no-man's land. He called God his Father and transgressed the law, being a friend of sinners and tax collectors. He called God his Father and became an outsider, and was executed as a criminal (*anomos*). So the people who followed him were right to call him the Son of this Father, for he was no one else's son or party member.

So if we want to know what it means to be 'a child of God', then we have to take our bearings from this unusual man from Nazareth. In brotherhood with him and in following his path to the cross we discover who God the Father is, and find what it means to be a child of this God on earth. From Jesus we discover, like the disciples, that for long enough we ourselves were only the enemies of our enemies, and are so still. But through him we discover even more the tremendous liberating power of love, which reaches us and disarms us, even when we are enemies.

The Sermon on the Mount was authenticated through its preacher. So it is not merely a lofty ideal. It is authenticated in us when we discover that he lived for us, suffered for us and died for us, while we were still enemies and godless (cf. Rom. 5.6,10), and when we live and love from this faith. Nor does God come to us by way of anything less than love for our enemy. God does not ask about good and evil, because even my good is not good before him. God's love seeks the enemy and is perfected in the enemy. If it were not for this, none of us could talk about God's love at all. Apart from this, none of us becomes the child of this God. This is the way Jesus, in his life and death, brought God to us. God's children are *enemies who have been overcome*. God's children live from a hard and costly love. It cost God the death of the Son. Through him, children of God are liberated from ever narrower spirals of hate in the heart and enmity in the world. They emerge from these prisons and see the sun of a new day, which rises in the morning over the evil and the good, making no distinction between them, but giving life and warmth to everyone. And everyone feels the rain which falls on the just and the unjust, and makes the wilderness of desolation fruitful again – without distinction and beyond good and evil.

These are great images, and they point to the sun of righteousness and the rain of life, which make good the evil of injustice, and overcome all infringements of justice. When the sun rises, we should cease struggling with the shadows of the night and should turn our faces to the light. When the rain comes, there is no longer any need to quarrel about water; we should rejoice in the rain with everyone else. How can this happen? Through love of our enemies. This kind of love is in profound accord with the nature of God. It corresponds to Jesus, right to the end. Through this love the Spirit of liberty enters into the midst of us. 'Love your enemies!' For God's sake, for Christ's sake, let us love our enemies! And that means seeing your enemy as your brother and treating him like your brother. Stop asking what he has *done* to you or to other people. Ask what he *suffers* from, and what the sufferings are which are turning him into your enemy. Ask what God wants to do for him – the God who lets his sun rise upon the evil and the good. Ask what Jesus has done for him. Love of the enemy is not a matter for weaklings who are afraid of that enemy. Anyone who is still afraid of his enemy does not know what love is. Love is only something for the person who has been liberated and who no longer lets himself be impressed by his opponent.

Love of one's enemy does not want to conquer him, or convert him to one's own views. This kind of love lives *together* with the enemy beneath God's sun, beyond good and evil. It carries him into this wider horizon. How?

'Bless those who curse you!' Cursing another person means wishing him in hell because one cannot bear his presence any longer. We all know the stronger curses and lesser terms of abuse we use for this. When they cannot stand you any more, when they damn you, then lift up your hands in blessing: you enemies, you who are blessed by God, go in peace! Let us stop slandering them and telling horror stories about them.

'Do good to those who hate you!' Doing good does not come about merely through words. It involves the things that are necessary for daily life. Give food and drink to the people who hate you. Help them wherever you can. Stand by them. Do not support your own interests against theirs. Support the interests you share. They are your brothers. These enemies are really the ones who are unhappy.

'Pray for those who insult and persecute you!' That is the final thing. 'Father forgive them, for they know not what they do,' Jesus

prayed when he was dying. In prayer, one person intercedes for the
other, takes the other's fear and hate on himself, stands beside him in
solidarity under the sun which rises on the evil and the good – and on
the evil first of all.

'Is this practicable? Can one live with it?' we ask yet again. Well,
Jesus himself called this the special thing, the thing that is extraordinary and abnormal. There is no difficulty about repaying like with
like. Everyone does this. We all do it every day, for good or ill. Loving
our friends and hating our enemies – this is the tune we dance to all
our life, tramping on the people we do not want to see. Birds of a
feather flock together. We can have this everywhere: in our clubs, in
our political parties, and unfortunately in the church of Christ too.
Everyone in his in-group cage. The person who is like myself gives me
confidence in what I am. Anyone who is different and wants something different makes me insecure.

Away with him! Away from him! How boring this is! Everyone
stewing in his own juice. But the person who is out of step – who likes
associating with different kinds of people and with people of different
beliefs – anyone who shelters the enemies of the state, the enemies of
his class, the enemies of his church, is soon at odds with the law.
Anyone who accepts conflicts and uses his imagination to overcome
them, anyone who tries to do the special thing, the unusual thing –
which means loving the enemies of his group and doing good to them
– that person has to suffer. He falls between all the different stools.
He is not at home anywhere any more. For the one person he is a
traitor, and for the other an uncertain quantity. Love of one's enemy
can be fatal, as we can see from the fate of Martin Luther King and
many other martyrs of our time. It needs endurance and strong nerves
to see this way through. It needs continually new liberation from the
vicious circles of fear and violence which attract us so strongly. It
needs the wide space of God's sun, which warms and sheds its light
on the evil and the good. Finally – and this is the price – it requires
acceptance of suffering. Love your enemies – the suffering of this
love is the most fruitful and the most liberating power. We learn the
meaning of this suffering from the passion of the preacher on the
Mount. We learn it from the suffering of the martyrs. We learn it,
too, both personally and politically, from Gandhi. Let me, in closing,
paraphrase some words of his, spoken during the Indian struggle for
liberty:

Not everything that is of fundamental significance for a people can be achieved by reason alone. It has to be bought by suffering. It may be that rivers of blood will have to flow before we are free; but then it must be our blood, not the blood of others. Suffering is a much stronger force than the law of the jungle; for suffering can transform our opponents too.

Intercession
Father, we pray for our enemies. Be gracious to them, bless them, accept them.

We pray for the enemies of the church, the enemies of faith and of your crucified Son. Peace be with them!

Be gracious to those who despise us and persecute us. Take fear and hate from our hearts. We pray for the enemies of our country and its political order. Peace be with them!

Graciously accept the people who find us unendurable, and awake love for them in our hearts. Give peace in the midst of conflict. Give love where people hate each other. May your kingdom come and the law of retaliation pass away. May your suffering transform us from enemies to friends, who can rejoice in one another in your peace.

8 The Transformation of Life

And after six days Jesus took with him Peter and James and John his brother, and led them up a high mountain apart. And he was transfigured before them, and his face shone like the sun, and his garments became white as light. And behold there appeared to them Moses and Elijah, talking with him. And Peter said to Jesus, 'Lord, it is well that we are here; if you wish, I will make three booths here, one for you and one for Moses and one for Elijah.' He was still speaking, when lo, a bright cloud overshadowed them, and a voice from the cloud said, 'This is my beloved Son, with whom I am well pleased; listen to him.' When the disciples heard this, they fell on their faces, and were filled with awe. But Jesus came and touched them, saying, 'Rise, and have no fear.' And when they lifted up their eyes, they saw no one but Jesus only. And as they were coming down the mountain, Jesus commanded them, 'Tell no one the vision, until the Son of man is raised from the dead' (Matt. 17.1–9).

Anyone who really lives his life with conscious awareness probably cherishes in some corner of his heart an undefined longing for deliverance: deliverance from tension, from uncomprehended suffering, from the daily demands of work and the claims made on us through our living together with other human beings. We want to escape from the emptiness of existence and attain a full life. We want to stop being irresolute and become clear about things. The more profoundly a person loves life and suffers it, the more strongly every day shows him that we are never finished. We are overtaxed. We are overburdened. We are unable to discover what the right thing is, and even when we discover, we are still unable to do it. Whatever decision we take, we fall short. We are imprisoned – nailed to our own omissions and incapacities.

So is it surprising that we should seek for deliverance and dream of happiness and fulfilled hopes, peace and safety? Is it to be wondered at that we should long for a different life, a life full of harmony and success? A life where we can laugh completely light-heartedly, where the world is again innocent and unscathed, free of hunger and fear, free of guilt and inexorable necessity?

Is it surprising if people for whom this one great longing for deliverance has been shattered in disappointment should then cling to the thousand little deliverances which we can still manufacture for ourselves?

So we continually seek for moments of happiness, the highlights of life – heights that tower up like mountain peaks above the sombre, toilsome plains of everyday life. With this aim, we snatch at every opportunity for a celebration; or we seize on the concerts where with the sound of music we can give ourselves up to the enchantment of a better, unscathed world. We 'draw' on hours like this long afterwards; they give us new energy to master life. We 'draw' on our holidays, or on the hour of success when we are borne up by a wave of recognition. Moments like this 'transfigure' life, give it a meaningful solemnity which it otherwise lacks.

Do not the church, worship and faith also belong to this sphere, where we can find new security and peace for our restless souls? These are words which do us good. They accompany us like faithful companions into the new week, the new page of life, the difficult decisions we have to face in the course of our duties.

Surely the goal of all our seekings and hopes is to find, once and again, the moment and the place where we can say with all our heart: 'It is well that we are here: let us make booths here!' Surely our purpose is to enjoy the moment to which we can cry, with Goethe's Faust, 'O tarry a while, thou art so fair!'

Of course we can easily understand the disciples, if it was just this that they had looked for with Jesus, so that now, on the Mount of Transfiguration, they broke into rejoicing. Now the hour of fulfilment had come! He took them 'up a high mountain apart', and a supernatural radiance, the transfiguring glory of God, surrounded him and them. How should they not draw a deep breath, like people who have finally found the thing they have long sought for? 'It is well that we are here; let us build booths here.' Let us forget the world down there with its pain. The peak of experience is here. This is where we want to stay. This hour of fulfilment must last for ever and ever, and must not be permitted to end. Here the heavens are open: Moses and Elijah, the great men of the nation's sublime past, appear and approach Jesus. All the gleams of hope from the past, all the signs that remind us of the future, seem to converge on a single focus: Jesus Christ, God's dwelling among men and women.

But what do the disciples really experience on the mountain? Why are they overcome by fear and dismay in this supreme moment?

What they experience is something different from the fulfilment of their longings. They are caught up in a complete reversal of events. What they have longed for is a flight from the difficulties and failures of life, to the mountain of bliss. But now they go back to the world, with Jesus. Their path does not end up there on the mountain. It turns back, down from the peak, away from the satisfying fulfilment of their own desires. It is a path that leads them to Jerusalem with Jesus, to suffering, beneath his cross.

What they longed for was to escape from the pressures of life, to be released from the problems and pains of this world, and to live a solitary existence away from other human beings. But what they are called to do is to live in the midst of this world: in its pains and problems, beneath the cross. They climb the mountain of their desire – and turn back to the place of their responsibility, which is beneath the cross, in the solidarity of love for human beings.

What happened to them? What gave their lives, their desires, feelings and thinking such a totally new direction?

Let us ask the disciples themselves. We put the question to them, because we somehow sense that the decisive act of our own lives would have to be governed by a similar revolution in our attitude. On the mountain the disciples experienced the miracle of Jesus' transfiguration. What was this transfiguration? They talk about it in the stammering, stuttering words we use when we are trying to make comprehensible something which is really totally unique. Luke says: 'The appearance of his countenance was altered, and his raiment became dazzling white.' Matthew reports: 'His face shone like the sun, and his garments became white as light.' And Mark: 'His garments became glistening, intensely white, as no fuller on earth could bleach them.' It is the radiance of God's perfection which descends on him and transforms him. The Old Testament tells us that Moses had encounters with God like this (Ex. 34), encounters which burst apart all known categories of understanding and comparison. In the Christmas story the angels appear in a similar way to the shepherds, like a blinding flash of lightning in the night: 'An angel of the Lord appeared to them, and the glory of the Lord shone around them, and they were filled with fear.' It is exactly this that the disciples experience here with Jesus. Perhaps we may say, 'Oh well, all right, it was a miracle. Like a fairy story.' But the question we ought rather to ask is: What is this sign intended to show us? When was Jesus transfigured in this way? Luke reports: 'As Jesus was praying.' As he prayed, turning to the 'Thou' of his life, his counterpart in God, his Father; as he sought him, opened his heart to him – it was then that what goes beyond human understanding happened. As he opened his existence to God in prayer his face was transformed, his being was transfigured. In the prayer of his heart he reflected the Father – his glory, his goodness, his clarity, his will.

Here we have to remember the attitude in which the Jews prayed: not with folded, clenched hands and bowed head, crouched and absorbed in themselves. They prayed with both hands raised and spread out towards heaven, with open eyes and upturned gaze. This, we have to suppose, was how Jesus stood before his disciples. As he stood like this, open body and soul for God, the brightness and reflection of God fell upon him, and was mirrored back from him again, not merely in his spirit but in his whole earthly being. He remained a man among men, his clothes remained human material, but as he prayed and the Father beheld him, his life shone like a mirror – like a reflector which in itself and by itself is nothing, until it throws back the light it receives – throws it back and throws it further and diffuses it round itself. That is the secret of Jesus.

There is an old Chinese proverb that says: 'He who looks upon himself does not shine.' And it is true: the person who looks at himself certainly does not shine. The person who thinks only of his own happiness and his own advancement spreads the suffocating atmosphere of a craving for life, and the hectic breath of the competitive struggle. I think we have all seen this look on distorted, tense, exhausted human faces.

Anyone who has a fixation about something and has nothing but this in mind certainly shines. But what he reflects is fanaticism. We are all familiar with the fanatic – his rigid features, his glassy eyes, the words that tumble over themselves, and the hands greedy for power.

A person always takes the stamp of the things he seeks and loves, the things he pursues and which pursue him. He always reflects the forces that possess him. And when a person has nothing he is prepared to do his utmost for, because it means more to him than anything on earth, then he reflects the distraction, the instability and the lack of purpose which has not unjustly been called the signature of our generation. 'For they know not what they do.'

Jesus' secret is that he reflects God alone and God completely. He is stamped as true human being wholly and entirely by God and by God alone. His secret manifests itself in the prayer that seeks the Father. Through this seeking prayer he opens himself to the Father's influence and conforms to his will. This story shows us in vivid, pictorial terms what is meant by saying that Jesus is the visible image of the invisible God. Jesus is God's Son. He makes visible to us what God intended when he created us to be his image. And he also finally manifests what we shall be together with him: God's friends, 'set free from bondage to decay, freed for the glorious liberty of the children of God' (Rom. 8.21). The voice the disciples hear from the clouds is simply an authentication of what Jesus is: 'This is my beloved Son, with whom I am well pleased; listen to him.' Jesus is God's human image. Jesus is God's Son for us, so that we may become his brothers and sisters.

Let us notice that *prayer* is the place where this relation to God finds its realization. The person who looks at himself – either in vanity or despair – does not shine. But in prayer the reflection of God's glory falls on the worshipper and transfigures him; for here a person forgets himself and yields up control over himself, looking simply to the Father. From the eternal 'Thou' of the Father, the human 'I' acquires its true life in a relationship of sonship, thereby taking on clarity and form.

Not through your gaze alone
do you perceive the world
or through your acts.
Only in prayer

your vision slowly changes
till the last veil falls (Rüdiger Syberberg).

As the disciples hear this voice of God they apprehend the truth of who Jesus really is. They are appalled, terror-stricken. They fall on their faces and dare not look upon the One who has been so transfigured before their eyes. And Jesus comes to them and lifts them up: 'Rise, and have no fear.' And when they raise their eyes they see no more heavenly visions. They see 'no one but Jesus'. *Him alone*, without any radiance or glory. They see nothing but his humanity, his lowliness. Jesus alone, as he prepares to set out on the way of obedience that leads to death on the cross. Now they are horrified because they do not merely discern who Jesus is; they also sense what the path is like that he has to tread and for which he is sent. It is not a path leading steadily upwards, from one splendid moment to the next. It is the path of descent, the path of faithfulness and obedience to death. It is not the way that fulfils human longings for a full, lovely and unscathed life. It is the road inexorably determined by the Father, the road that leads him to that other mountain, to the hour of forsakenness, to the exaltation which was the exaltation of the cross. In prayer Jesus was transfigured before their eyes in the reflection of the Father. In obedience he endured this transfiguration to the point of inescapable suffering, to the point of what was, humanly speaking, a meaningless death.

The disciples have closed their eyes to a future like this. When they open them they see nothing except Jesus. Nothing more of their dreams of deliverance, nothing more of divine radiance, away from the world on a high mountain. Nothing except the Jesus who in obedience fulfils the will of God in this world. And to this Jesus they listen. It is him that they follow.

Now, no night is so dark that the light of transfiguration does not fall on the person who takes up his cross and seeks the will of God along the path of Jesus.

Now, no suffering – neither the suffering we impose on ourselves nor the suffering inflicted by other people – is so unendurable nor any guilt so unacceptable that, with Jesus, the profound 'Yes' of faith cannot be found: 'Yes, Father, not my will but thine be done, on earth as it is in heaven, and so in me too.'

The transfiguration of life is not found in escape, or in dreams of harmony, but only in this 'yes' of self-surrender and obedience. Where the will of the Father is fulfilled in us and for us and through us – there life is transfigured; even in the face of tears and pain and disappointment.

Do we know now where to find life's 'great moments'? Do we know now what moments will be good and full of satisfaction?

We shall not find them at the point where we escape from the pressures of life, avoid decision, flee into oblivion, and dream away our lives – apart on a high mountain.

The great moments are the ones when, with Jesus, we take up our cross, when with him we descend and enter into the world's suffering, into temptation and into bodily obedience. For here we shall be brought into harmony with the will of God.

Where God's will finds its echo and response in our human weakness, when it is met by an obedient 'yes' out of the depths – even if it is perhaps only a small 'yes', a trembling 'yes', perhaps only a weary and doubtful 'yes' – then that person is transfigured, then the divine splendour falls on him, then the divine sonship shines in the midst of the tensions and wretchedness of this world. The person who knows Jesus for what he is, and has faith in him, will lose the tormenting longings of his heart and take on instead the unforgettable impress of the charge he has been given.

None of us will be *delivered* from the world, but we shall all be *chosen* for this world.

'They saw no one but Jesus.' How should we have anything else in view? Where else should we find the light that transfigures our life? No one but Jesus; and they went down with him. So let us go down with him too, into the failings of our life and into the poverty of our world. We shall find him there. It is there that God is waiting for us.

9 Liberating Mission

And Jesus returned in the power of the Spirit into Galilee, and a report concerning him went out through all the surrounding country. And he taught in their synagogues, being glorified by all. And he came to Nazareth, where he had been brought up; and he went to the synagogue, as his custom was, on the sabbath day. And he stood up to read; and there was given to him the book of the prophet Isaiah. He opened the book and found the place where it was written (Isa. 61.1,2): 'The Spirit of the Lord is upon me, because he has anointed me to preach good news to the poor. He has sent me to proclaim release to the captives and recovering of sight to the blind, to set at liberty those who are oppressed, to proclaim the acceptable year of the Lord.'

And he closed the book, and gave it back to the attendant, and sat down; and the eyes of all in the synagogue were fixed on him. And he began to say to them, 'Today this scripture has been fulfilled in your hearing' (Luke 4.14–21).

Mission is participation in the mission of Jesus. Mission is 'the feast with Jesus'. Everything that is done and suffered abroad in Africa, Asia and Latin America by missionaries, clergy, evangelists, doctors, people engaged in works of charity, and development-aid volunteers takes place in Jesus' name and in participation in his own mission. Everything that happens here among us, in and through the community of Christians, in preaching, fellowship and service, takes place in Jesus' name and is participation in his own mission. Today's worship and today's sermon, too, are subject to the assurance that

'Today – this morning – this scripture has been fulfilled in our hearing.'

Mission is the all-comprehending mandate to which the whole Christian community is called. But none of us can fulfil this mandate, and subject his own life to it, unless he has previously heard its message; unless he himself has first been touched by Jesus' own mission and unless that mission has already been fulfilled in him. One cannot wish to act as missionary to other people if one is not prepared to accept the mission to oneself first. Jesus wants to be effective in us ourselves. And he fulfils his mission in us wherever the poor hear the gospel, the blind see, prisoners are liberated, and we all celebrate the feast of freedom with Jesus. Where we have this experience, we can and should pass it on to others, and in the same way: we should bring the gospel to the poor, free prisoners, let the blind see and the deaf hear, and begin the feast of freedom with other people.

Mission is participation in Jesus' own messianic mission – no more, and no less. Jesus' mission is the reason for ours, and defines our mandate and our potentialities. So we have continually to test our aims and methods against Jesus' own mission. For it is his mission and his alone, not ours.

There have been periods in the church when people went far beyond the mission of Jesus. People wanted to set up the kingdom of God on earth: Christian emperors and Christian armies subjugated heathen peoples and forced them to be baptized. This is what happened to our Germanic ancestors. In the last century, the 'white' nations subjected Africa and Asia to a 'Christian civilization' and set up colonial dominions. This kind of mission was carried on by way of blood and tears, the slave trade and other kinds of exploitation. It was not the gospel of freedom; it was the sword of oppression. Today the guilt of it lies heavy on our consciences.

And yet, on the other hand, participation in Jesus' mission cannot go far enough. After the arrogance of those years, and the heritage of guilt they left with us, many people today have become despondent, weary and lacking in faith. Many of us no longer expect anything of the proclamation of the gospel, and think that development aid and charitable projects are enough. They believe in 'share and share alike', but they fail to pass on the message of Jesus himself to other people. So this failure too lies heavy on our consciences today.

Whatever we may think about the one method or the other, the only important thing is that Jesus himself, with his mission, should be among us and then, through us, also make his influence felt in other people.

The time of mission is the messianic time

Whether mission is outmoded or not today is not something to be decided on the basis of our experience and our ideas. It is a question that has to be tested against the Messiah, Jesus himself.

The messianic time is God's time – 'the acceptable year of the Lord', as our Bible translates it – the year pleasing to God – the fulfilment of the promises of the prophets, as we find them in the scriptures, the fulfilment of the prisoners' hope for liberty, the hope for peace cherished by people living in conflict, the hope for God's coming which is the hope of the godforsaken.

The messianic time is God's today: today, as we hear the scripture, and as Jesus comes to us. How does this happen?

The story begins very simply: Jesus' ministry begins at home, so to speak. He comes to his home town Nazareth. As usual, he goes to his synagogue on the Sabbath. Just as we came to church this morning. Nothing special. As is the custom among the Jews, he stands up to read the congregation a passage of scripture. As is also usual, he is brought the scroll of scripture he asks for, and reads aloud what the prophet Isaiah said about the promised Messiah. According to Luke, he interpolates into Isa. 61. 1 and 2 the promise 'and recovery of sight to the blind', and breaks off the reading before the threat 'and the day of vengeance of our God'. Then he closes the scroll, sits down, and says to his expectant hearers, whose eyes are upon him, just one brief sentence – that is his whole sermon: '*Today this scripture has been fulfilled in your hearing.*'

This is unheard of. This changes everything. In the first place, there is the *today*. The prophet Isaiah had given hope to the poor, imprisoned and oppressed people who were in exile in Babylon: Behold, your God is coming. He will come and liberate the prisoners and lead the forsaken home again to Zion. Then the eyes of the blind will be opened, the lame will walk, the deaf will hear, the dumb will praise God. Then the feast of the Lord will begin – a feast without end. This is what is going to happen at God's coming. But as long as the poor do not hear the gospel, as long as the blind are blind, the prisoners still captive, and this world is as unredeemed as we know it to be, it is still night and not day, winter and not spring. So until that day we must wait patiently.

Jesus announces the time of fulfilment: *the hour has come.* 'The kingdom of God is at hand.' The night is far advanced, your day is dawning. Where? And when? Today, here, in your hearing. Jesus puts the messianic time into force. That is his mission. So the messianic time is Jesus' time. Jesus makes possible what we certainly hope for in our hearts, but have rationally always considered to be impossible: the blind see, the lame walk, the dead rise, the message of peace is brought to the poor. This is the first thing Jesus demands of his hearers: this *today* filled with enthusiasm, literally possessed by the divine Spirit.

If the first astonishing thing is the 'today', the second is *Jesus himself.* The people in the synagogue at Nazareth were surprised at his unprecedented words, and even more at the anything but overwhelming figure he presented. If he had appeared with a flourish, as a fantastic miracle-worker, or a victorious general, or a political leader, people might perhaps have believed his 'today'. But who was he, after all? 'Is this not Joseph's son?' the people in Nazareth asked ironically. A working-class boy, one of us? And though of course we are waiting for the Messiah, we are certainly no Messiahs ourselves. What good thing can come out of Nazareth? Or the small town or city suburb we happen to live in? A poor man as Messiah of the poor, a vulnerable man as saviour of the wounded, a powerless man as liberator of the helpless – nobody could expect that. We do not expect it either. It was this that brought Jesus to the cross. But the person who listens finds in the suffering and death of Jesus the fulfilment of his messianic mission, not its contradiction: '*Today* you will be with me in paradise', he says to the person who confesses his guilt and accepts his judgment. From the 'today' at the beginning in Nazareth, the road leads to the 'today' at the end, on the cross; and as the risen liberator he comes to us 'today' in word and Spirit. It is a 'today' that never ends, and on which night never again falls. It is the presence of the coming God, the feast without end. Because on the cross Jesus takes the judgment on himself, he leaves the threat 'and the day of vengeance of our God' out of his reading. Because on the cross he suffered judgment on our behalf, eternal life is open to us.

The messianic time is 'the acceptable year of the Lord'

Jesus' proclamation puts the acceptable year of the Lord into force. 'Acceptable' means what is agreeable to God – his good pleasure. It is therefore the year when he does good to us, the year of his grace. The acceptable year of the Lord is the time of salvation. The disastrous years of poverty, imprisonment and blindness are passing away; the year of salvation is coming. That is the one point. The Book of Leviticus tells us that the people of Israel celebrated a 'year of release' every fiftieth year, in which they rejoiced in quite material terms over the coming Day of God. On Yom Kippur, the Day of Atonement, after forty-nine years of struggle and labour, the trumpet of rejoicing was to be sounded, to announce the beginning of the Year of Jubilee. 'Then each of you shall return to his property and each of you shall return to his family.' Debts were remitted. People who had been imprisoned for debt were set at liberty, and slaves were freed. God's right to people and land was reasserted once again. The land, too, was to be left free of human seedtime and harvest, so that it could breathe again. The 'year of release' celebrated the divine joy over the mutual reconciliation and liberation of men and women. 'The acceptable year of the Lord' which is fulfilled in our hearing through Jesus' message is therefore a true liberation of the whole of life: soul and body, the individual and the community, human beings and nature. In its history of struggle and suffering, Israel hardly ever had an opportunity of celebrating this year of liberation. And so the prophets linked the Year of Jubilee with their hope for the coming Messiah. When God comes, the Year of Jubilee will begin. And God comes to us in and through Jesus.

In 1973, the Taizé slogan for its forthcoming Council of Youth was 'The Feast with Jesus', and Roger Schutz wrote about it:

> Jesus makes life a feast without end. The feast with Jesus is celebrated wherever a soul is freed of its guilt; it is celebrated whenever prisoners become free; wherever people whose rights have been taken from them acquire their rights as people once more; wherever the handicapped are accepted by the healthy; wherever a ghetto is dissolved, or a war ended.

The whole of life as a feast of liberation: even my defeats, even my grief, even my death? Yes. If the master of the feast is the crucified

Lord, even life's shadows belong to this feast of freedom. We no longer need to be ashamed of our tears, our mourning and our guilt. I believe Taizé grasped the mission of Jesus and 'the acceptable year of the Lord'. Jesus' message is the exultant trumpet call that proclaims God's year of Jubilee to the whole land. Here we are no longer subject to the laws that condemn us to poverty, imprisonment, blindness and guilt. What counts here is liberty, for here Jesus rules. Do we hear the trumpet? Does our feast with Jesus begin today?

Who are the people to whom it applies? The people mentioned are the prisoners, the blind and the oppressed; and it is all summed up in the phrase, 'the gospel to the poor'.

When Israel was forced to go into exile in Babylon, some people remained behind in their own country. The victors did not bother about them. They were 'the riff-raff' – the have-nothings, the sick, agricultural labourers – ordinary working-class people. When the prophets talk about the poor they are generally thinking of this despised group. In Jesus' time it meant the poverty-stricken, semi-enslaved country population. In Jesus' preaching it means the poor in the social sense – the sick, the handicapped, lepers – but also the unimportant people and the children, the stupid and the helpless, sinners, tax-collectors and whores. In Luke 7.22 the dead are included too.

The poor are all the people who have to put up with violence and injustice without being able to defend themselves. The poor are all the people who have to exist on the very fringe of death, with nothing to live from and nothing to live for. But in Jesus' message the poor are surely all of us too, since we have nothing to offer the coming God except the burden of our guilt and the rags of our exile – like the Prodigal Son.

In Jesus' proclamation 'the acceptable year of the Lord' is coming 'today'. And it is coming in quite practical terms, bringing everyone what he needs in his poverty, if he is to be free. To the prisoners it brings liberation, to the blind sight, to the deaf hearing, to the oppressed relief, to the dead the resurrection. That is why we read at the beginning: 'The Spirit of the Lord is upon me.' For this Spirit is the Spirit of life, the power of creation, the power of the resurrection. This Spirit and this power continually conveys to us, in the mission of Jesus, signs and tokens of what is to come. Wherever we hear the

Word of the joy of God, wherever a mourner is comforted or a sick person is healed, wherever prisoners are set free, wherever we experience love – there we sense the energies of the Spirit, and there the feast of freedom *begins*. But it is only *fulfilled*, only reaches its climax in the resurrection of the dead. Jesus opens our whole life for this future. So we can be poor, sick, grieving and cast down – and yet already stand in the joy of God and participate in the feast of freedom. Once the Liberator has come, the liberations cannot be far off. And when we fail because, instead of love, we meet with contempt – when, instead of liberation, we see only new oppression – then we will hold fast to him and remember his word. 'All the works of God have their hidden beginnings in the word, but their end in deeds and wonders.'

Mission is participation in the mission of Jesus. The messianic era is the era of mission. The poor have the gospel preached to them. Liberty is brought to the imprisoned, the broken and the oppressed. The blind see, the lame walk, the deaf hear, and the feast of freedom begins. This is the mission of Jesus. This – in faith in him – is the mission of the community of Christians, too. The new creation begins wherever the Spirit and the energies of the Spirit are alive. That is why in I Corinthians 12 Paul sets the whole church and every individual Christian in the framework of the sending – the mission – of the Spirit. The gifts and energies of the Spirit vary. They are as motley as creation itself. Everyone in his own way is given his share in the presence of the Lord that makes us free. In the Spirit my whole life, my soul and my body, my energies and my potentialities, are put at the service of Jesus' mission, become part of the feast of freedom. Nothing is too high, nothing is too low. No one is too good for this and no one is too obscure. A widow is just as important as a bishop. Someone who shows mercy is no more insignificant than a preacher of the gospel. Everyone, each in his own place, is to keep the feast with Jesus and bring liberation to the world.

This means that active hands should not despise the speaking lips, and the listening ear should not despise the running feet. The whole body of Christ should work together. There are many energies, but only one Spirit; many gifts, but only one Lord; many ways, but only one common future.

It seems to me that there is a great deal of unnecessary dispute today about which function is the most important. Everyone wants to play first violin, to lead the orchestra in the concert celebrating the

feast with Jesus. Let us put this dispute aside. Everyone should do
what is within his own capacity, in his own place and with all his
energies, to serve the mission of Jesus and the feast of freedom in the
world. If one travels round the world nowadays, Christianity often
appears to be very variegated and very disunited. One church centres
on the liturgy, another on preaching, another on the sacraments, yet
another on works of charity. Here we find apolitical Christians, there
Christians who are deeply involved in politics. But if we think about
it, this shows the wealth of the church, not its poverty. Why should
we not learn from one another? Why should we not bury our mutual
mistrust? Everywhere and in every congregation there are so many
dormant, unawakened gifts and powers which God wants to use for
his mission. So why do we try to quench the Spirit? Not everyone has
to preach, not everyone has to administer the affairs of the congregation, but everyone should participate with all his powers in the
feast of freedom. I believe that it is the task of the gathered congregation to see to it that everyone finds his own particular role and
function in the great divine movement for liberation on the way to
the resurrection, when death will be swallowed up in victory.

Jesus' earthly ministry began at home in Nazareth, and then spread
in ever-widening ripples until it reached its goal in Jerusalem. His
ministry in the Spirit began in Jerusalem, then, in ever-widening
ripples, to spread to the ends of the earth and the ends of time.

Today mission also begins 'at home', here in this congregation,
and 'today', when the scripture is fulfilled in our hearing. And then
it begins to ripple out, over the frontiers – over the political frontiers
to far-off lands, over the frontiers of race, caste and class to the poor.

I never used to know exactly what a 'missionary festival' was
supposed to be. Why a festival? Were we supposed to celebrate
conversions? But today I know what it is. A missionary festival is 'the
feast with Jesus', the feast of liberation in the acceptable year of the
Lord; and I am certain that it is a feast without end.

10 The Consequences of Discipleship

I tell you, my friends, do not fear those who kill the body, and after that have no more that they can do. But I will warn you whom to fear: fear him who, after he has killed, has power to cast into hell; yes, I tell you, fear him!

Are not five sparrows sold for two pennies? And not one of them is forgotten before God. Why, even the hairs of your head are all numbered. Fear not; you are of more value than many sparrows.

And I tell you, every one who acknowledges me before men, the Son of man also will acknowledge before the angels of God; but he who denies me before men will be denied before the angels of God. And every one who speaks a word against the Son of man will be forgiven; but he who blasphemes against the Holy Spirit will not be forgiven.

And when they bring you before the synagogues and the rulers and the authorities, do not be anxious how or what you are to answer or what you are to say; for the Holy Spirit will teach you in that very hour what you ought to say (Luke 12.4–12).

The idea of discipleship is a Cinderella of Protestantism, especially in the established churches. Ever since Luther's time, the idea of discipleship and its practice has been left to the 'voluntary' groups on the left wing of the Reformation – the people who were notoriously slandered as 'enthusiasts', 'fanatics', 'do-gooders' or 'radicals'. It was really Dietrich Bonhoeffer who made the word fit for polite society with his book, *The Cost of Discipleship*. That was forty years ago, at the time of the Confessing Church and its struggle. 'Cheap grace is the deadly enemy of our church,' he wrote in 1938. 'Cheap grace is grace without discipleship, grace without the cross, grace without Christ.' Costly grace, on the other hand, is 'grace that calls to discipleship'. It is costly because it can cost a person his life. 'It is grace because it leads him into true life.'

The student congregation was evidently thinking of this when it thought of having this series of sermons on 'The Consequences of Discipleship'. By doing so it has put preachers and listeners – and perhaps itself too – in rather a difficult position. For one thing, we seem seldom to take as sermon texts the biblical passages on the subject of discipleship which have been chosen. For another thing, we have to look back a long way, or range afield over other countries, to find examples illustrating the experience of discipleship and its consequences for personal life. Most of us therefore have as little desire for Christian discipleship as we have for its consequences. We would rather take upon ourselves the consequences of avoided, denied, rejected discipleship. And these consequences are lack of assurance in faith, the guilty fear our consciences feel, and the despondent anxiety in which we live. And when one or another group of Christians does choose the way of radical discipleship, they are immediately stamped as 'enthusiasts', 'fanatics', 'do-gooders' or 'radicals'. They are forced on to the fringes of society – and the church. Our bad consciences see to that. No, the conditions to which we have become accustomed are certainly anything but favourable to the idea and practice of discipleship. Is this not obvious from the very fact that discipleship of Christ seems to us an unreasonable imposition, and that – as the subject chosen by this student congregation shows – we immediately take a sideways glance at the cost of discipleship, or its consequences? But the person who really enters upon Christian discipleship looks to the One who accompanies him and goes ahead of him. He looks at the promise and future of discipleship. He does not glance timidly over his shoulder at the consequences. 'Discipleship is joy' – the joy of faith, joy over the coming kingdom. And non-discipleship must then surely mean sadness. So let us look at the consequences of *non*-discipleship and compare them with the promise given to Christ's followers.

Of whom have I to be afraid?

'Do not fear those who kill the body, and after that have no more that they can do,' says Jesus. And he says it to people whom he explicitly calls his friends. Friends are bound together by affection and respect – and liberty. One makes no pretence to one's friends. The whole truth is *the imposition* one can expect one's friends to put up with. And the person who imposes this on his friends here, in this passage, knows what he is talking about. He speaks from experience. He knows himself what it means to fall into the hands of people who can 'kill the body'. So we can surely trust what he says. Here Jesus is talking about the experience of the martyrs. His own Jewish history was, and still is, to a great extent a history of martyrdom. Hebrews 11.36ff. tells us what it means to be able to kill the body:

> Some were tortured, refusing to accept release, that they might rise again to a better life. Others suffered mocking and scourging, and even chains and imprisonment. They were stoned, they were sawn in two, they were killed with the sword; they went about in skins of sheep and goats, destitute, afflicted, ill-treated – of whom the world was not worthy – wandering over deserts and mountains, and in dens and caves of the earth.

And why? What did they get out of it? 'All these God acknowledged.'

'Those who kill the body': that does not simply apply to your own life. It also means the people who can obstruct, hurt and kill your family, your wife, your children, and who try to blackmail you by this means.

This is not something belonging to the far-away past. It is happening round about us every day. We can see that from the tortured, maimed, imprisoned witnesses in central America, Uganda, South Korea; from the blackmailed, humiliated, imprisoned witnesses in the countries ruled by socialism 'in its actually existing form'; from the Jewish witnesses to righteousness who have been despised and murdered for centuries – by us as well. This is reality – the everyday reality experienced by witnesses to Christ. Only the person who deliberately keeps his eyes shut can be blind to this. But we see it and know it. We have certainly to cry out and accuse. But even more we have to ask for courage not to be afraid of it all.

Here Jesus first of all drives out one fear by means of another. 'Do not be afraid of human beings. They can only kill the body, nothing else. But be afraid of God, who can destroy body and soul, and cast you into hell.' This sounds strange. Is it an account to be settled in the next world? I do not think so. I think it is a clear calculation of the cost of discipleship, set against the cost of non-discipleship. The consequences of forgotten, denied and rejected discipleship really are the torments of hell. They show themselves in this world in the faith that has become unsure, in the guilty fears of conscience, and in the moral backbone broken for ever.

This is not merely a personal experience, which everyone goes through with his lies, his anxiety and his cowardice. It is a collective experience, too. Let me remind you of the inconceivable silence of the churches and the great majority of Christians in Germany forty years ago, when the synagogues went up in flames and the mass murder of Jewish witnesses to the righteousness of God began. I remind you of this as someone touched by the consequences of that silence, not as accuser.

One man cried out at that time. It was von Jan, the pastor of Oberlenningen in Württemberg. On Repentance Day, a week after that night of government-sanctioned crime, he put himself on the side of the Jews and preached: 'Where in Germany is . . . the man who cries out in God's name and in the name of righteousness, as Jeremiah did: execute justice and righteousness, and deliver the spoiled out of the hand of the oppressor! And do no wrong, do no violence, to the stranger, the fatherless, nor the widow, neither shed innocent blood in this place.' And he cried: 'Passions have been unleashed, the commandments of God ignored, houses of God which were sacred to others have been burnt down unpunished, the property of others robbed or destroyed.' For this, Pastor von Jan was beaten up by the SA, thrown into prison and expelled from Württemberg. The leaders of the church did not protect him. They merely censured him for encumbering his preaching with 'political remarks'. It must be added that later Bishop Wurm saw this attitude on the part of the church leaders as unforgivable guilt, and suffered profoundly under it. He never got over it until the day of his death. But what Reinhold Schneider wrote is true: 'On the day when the synagogues were attacked, the churches should have stood beside the synagogues as their brothers. The fact that they did not do so is crucial.'

We have not just to accuse ourselves, and confess our guilt because what should have been done then was not done. What is more important is to struggle, even today, with the appalling results of non-discipleship during those years: with the continual unconscious repression of that failure, with the continual unconscious compensating of guilty fear through an obtrusive self-righteousness, and with lost credibility, a lost assurance of faith and our own self-confidence in that faith. 'Repression hinders redemption. Remembrance brings it closer,' is written on the memorial in Jerusalem to the six million murdered Jews. It is a truth that applies to us Germans even more. The consequences of non-discipleship – the consequences of truth repudiated, justice shattered, humanity betrayed – are catastrophic, both in our church and in our nation. Repudiated truth and betrayed humanity leave behind them people who are open to blackmail, opportunist and without principle – people who no longer know themselves for what they are. This is a personal challenge that faces us in everyday life, and not just in highly exceptional cases. If I deny the truth, if I permit injustice, if I take no notice of the people who are being persecuted – then my family and I will get along the better for it; but the torments of hell begin at the same time – the torments of a broken backbone and unforgivable guilt.

If I confess the truth, if I fight for righteousness, if I put myself on the side of the persecuted, then I myself shall be isolated. I shall have to put up with slights, and my children will have to suffer for it too; but we shall have the infinite joy of being able to walk upright and hold our heads high. We have to choose. And we choose every minute. So let us be clear about the question: what have we to fear more, the consequences of discipleship or the consequences of non-discipleship?

'Do not fear those who kill the body, and after that have no more that they can do. Fear him who has power to cast into hell; yes, I tell you, fear him!'

The promise given to discipleship: Fear not!

'Are not five sparrows sold for two pennies? And not one of them is forgotten before God. Why, even the hairs of your head are all numbered. So fear not!' Now one fear is no longer expelled by another. Here fear is overcome by *trust*. God knows those who are his, and does not forget them. That is what the comparison with the little sparrows means. And if not even a single hair falls from our head without God's willing it to be so, then no one and nothing can tear us out of God's hand.

This certainty is the promise given to discipleship. But it is a certainty that only comes *through* discipleship. And it emerges with overwhelming force in the pains of that discipleship. I am safe in God. I am unassailable. I shall not fall. I am absolutely sure.

Here Jesus does not promise that we shall be spared the consequences of discipleship. No protection is promised for the body they can kill, the family they can blackmail, the profession they can forbid. Yet we are protected *in* all these consequences. God never loses sight of his friends. None of them will be lost to him. And *God* is with his friends. What happens to them happens *to him*. He goes to prison *with* them. The person who in his confession of Christ exposes himself so vulnerably in trust like this – the true witness – is a person who is profoundly secure. Whatever besets him, threatens him, blackmails and persecutes him, fails to touch him in his inmost being. At some point in his heart or soul he is unassailable, untouchable, unconquerable and serene. He is the master of the situation.

I have often wanted a serene confidence like this – to be able to go through life without fear or cravenness, and always to do the right thing unflinchingly. But I have never achieved it. Why not? I suppose because I have always loved life too much, and do so still. Must not everything be a matter of equal indifference if one wants to go through life as freely and unconcernedly as this?

The wandering philosophers of the ancient world, the famous Stoics, taught *ataraxia*, fearlessness. One achieves this fearlessness if one is totally indifferent; and one is only totally indifferent if everything is a matter of indifference. I have never found this indifference possible; so I have never achieved Stoic heroism – and probably never really wanted to.

But what kind of fearlessness does the gospel mean? Safe-keeping in God is not security in the chill of one's own heart. It is safe-keeping in another. 'If God is for us, who can be against us?' and, 'Nothing can separate us from the love of God which is in Christ Jesus', says Paul. This, and only this, is Christian assurance.

If this is the eternal foundation of our trust in God in this temporal life, then this foundation is certainly unassailable. No one can take it from us. But can we really be so certain of our own trust in God? When he leads us into persecution and imprisonment and whatever follows, shall we not curse God and deny Christ and forswear our faith if we are asked to do so, simply for the sake of being released? After all, our hearts are not made of stone and our characters are anything but rock-like.

In the New Testament we find the story of the disciple on whose faith Jesus wanted to build his church. The disciple is called a rock: Peter. But when he was faced with enduring the consequences of discipleship, he preferred to choose the consequences of denial. He denied Jesus three times. The cock crowed, and Peter went out and wept bitterly. That is not a model for people confessing their faith. It is certainly not an unshakeable rock. And yet it was to this very person that Jesus said: 'Simon, Simon, Satan demanded to have you, that he might sift you like wheat, but I have prayed for you that your faith may not fail' (Luke 22.31f.). Peter denies Jesus, and for him that means the end of his faith. Yet that faith of his does not end after all. For it lives in *Christ's intercession*, and out of that intercession it wakes to new life again. This is the unconquerable thing in faith: '*I have prayed for you.*'

I am not sure of myself. I do not know how long I can endure. I do not know when I shall weaken. I am not a rock. In fact I am more or less certain that I am going to fall. But I am more certain still that I can get up again when I have fallen; that nothing – not even my irreparable guilt – can keep me down. The confidence in God which gives us this tremendous sense of being in safe-keeping does not save us from outward shame and inward defeat; but it does give us the strength to get up again after every defeat, and to continue our resistance. The safe-keeping in Christ from which faith lives is safe-keeping in the power of the resurrection. 'We are afflicted in every way, but not crushed,' says Paul, and goes on, 'perplexed but not driven to despair; persecuted but not forsaken.' We are certainly not the stuff heroes are made of, but we do not give up. Why not? It would be so much easier. Because we have not been given up ourselves. God never gives us up – never, in any circumstances.

The acknowledgment of Jesus Christ

'Every one who acknowledges me before men, the Son of man also will acknowledge before the angels of God; but he who denies me

before men will be denied before the angels of God.' Discipleship
means acknowledgment, and acknowledgment means discipleship.
So non-discipleship means denial, and denial non-discipleship. Both
have consequences for eternity, and eternity has consequences for
what we say and fail to say here. I find it a relief that in the first place
Christ is the subject of the acknowledgment. He acknowledges us
before God. He is our witness in the judgment. He speaks for us
when we ourselves would have to be silent out of shame. He intervenes
on our behalf when we would have to sink into the ground. He is our
witness. He is our witness entirely and wholly, in word and deed,
with his faithfulness to death.

The witness and discipleship of believers are determined by the
witness and self-giving of Christ. His witness was public, so the
acknowledgment of Christians too is public, and not private. The
cause of Christ, which is truth and righteousness, is not 'a private
matter', like modern religion.

His witness is entire and whole, so the witness of Christians too is
entire and whole. Any restriction to the sphere of 'inwardness' or 'the
religious life' – with the exclusion of politics, at least – divides Christ
and leads to denial of him, and to the consequences of non-discipleship. The Christian witness is always 'encumbered by political
remarks' if its aim is to be *undividedly* Christian.

Christian witness is not merely verbal acknowledgment. It is the
witness of a life lived in discipleship. No confessing faith without
practical discipleship; no practical discipleship without unequivocal
confession. How is Christ confessed today, and how are we to follow
him? What or whom should I specifically acknowledge? That is the
question. Where is Christ present today? Christ is present and awaits
our acknowledgment of him:

in the gospel;
in the community of his people;
in the poor and oppressed.

We can pass him by if we do not hear his liberating message of the
kingdom. We can pass him by if we are ashamed of the community
of his people. We pass him by when we pass by people who are
hungry, thirsty, naked, sick and imprisoned. 'As you did it to one of
the least of these my brethren, you did it to me', we read in Matthew
25, in the great judgment of the Son of Man.

Was he – the Son of Man, who judges and saves – not among us forty years ago, in the hungry, thirsty, plundered, sick and imprisoned Jews? Did we not deny him in them? Is he – the Son of Man, who judges and saves – not among us today in the hungry, thirsty, destitute, sick and imprisoned people in the so-called Third World? If one reads the dry statistics, which talk about ten million deaths every year from hunger, most of them children, in that Third World, then one can be overcome by the same horror as overwhelmed us in 1945. Shall we and our children one day stand incredulously before this fact, as we did once before, when we were faced with the pictures of Auschwitz and Bergen-Belsen?

Every one who acknowledges me before men, the Son of man will acknowledge before the angels of God. He who denies me, him also will I deny before the angels of God.

So let us for God's sake do something courageous! Choose the hope of discipleship whatever the consequences may be! Avoid the consequences of non-discipleship, for they bring nothing but despair!

May God keep us on the path of discipleship. May Christ keep our faith alive. May the Spirit reveal to us what we should say and do.

11 The Pharisee and the Tax Collector

Vindicate me, O Lord, for I have walked in my integrity, and I have trusted in the Lord without wavering. Prove me, O Lord, and try me; test my heart and my mind. For thy steadfast love is before my eyes, and I walk in faithfulness to thee. I do not sit with false men, nor do I consort with dissemblers; I hate the company of evildoers, and I will not sit with the wicked. I wash my hands in innocence, and go about thy altar, O Lord, singing aloud a song of thanksgiving, and telling all thy wondrous deeds. O Lord, I love the habitation of thy house, and the place where thy glory dwells. Sweep me not away with sinners, nor my life with bloodthirsty men, men in whose hands are evil devices, and whose right hands are full of bribes. But as for me, I walk in my integrity; redeem me, and be gracious to me. My foot stands on level ground; in the great congregation I will bless the Lord (Ps. 26, 'The Pharisee's Psalm').

Text
Two men went up into the temple to pray, one a Pharisee and the other a tax collector. The Pharisee stood and prayed thus with himself, 'God, I thank thee that I am not like other men, extortioners, unjust, adulterers, or even like this tax collector. I fast twice a week, I give tithes of all that I get.' But the tax collector, standing far off, would not even lift up his eyes to heaven, but beat his breast, saying, 'God, be merciful to me a sinner!' I tell you, this man went down to his house justified rather than the other (Luke 18.10–14).

Luke reports that Jesus told this parable 'to certain people who trusted in themselves that they were righteous and despised others'. If we want to understand the parable and experience its healing effect on ourselves, we must stop looking round elsewhere for these 'certain people who trusted in themselves'. We – you and I – are these people ourselves. The story tells that two people once went to the temple, quite by chance at the same time. They did not know each other personally, but they were well enough known in Jerusalem as typical of certain groups. The one was a Pharisee, the other a tax collector. The one was a good man, the other a real crook. The one led a decent moral and religious life. The other was mixed up in dirty business. The Pharisee belonged to the group of people who were active in religious and social affairs. He knew what the essential thing in life is: to do the will of God according to the law. He knew what is important in human society: the distinction between good and evil. The middle classes, honest working people, and people who were trying to rise in the social scale, all followed this honourable and respectable discipline. Tax collectors were more or less at the other end of Jerusalem society. These men were collaborationists with the Roman occupying power. To put it bluntly, they were traitors to their country. By demanding higher taxes than were actually due, they made sure of their own cut. To put it bluntly again, their business was corruption.

We have all come to church, to our temple, this morning. Most of us do not know one another personally but the types we represent are of course well enough known in the town. In the parable the local colouring is taken from Jerusalem society. In this congregation the colouring belongs to the local newspaper. I imagine that few of us are as good, as noble, or as honourable as the Pharisee in the story. But I do not suppose that many of us are as repellent as the corrupt tax collector. Each of us is a mixture somewhere between the two, part Pharisee, part tax collector; sometimes a Pharisee, sometimes a tax collector. This is what we are known to be – known to other people and known to ourselves. But who are we really? Who knows our Pharisee's soul and who knows our tax collector's soul? Who is going to heal the conflict within us and among us?

Those two men, then, typical examples of Jerusalem society, went to the temple to pray. It is there, in the way they present themselves to God, that Jesus pins them down and pronounces judgment on them. *In prayer* the two men reveal themselves before God Almighty. Under the heaven of his Law they present what they think is the truth about themselves; the one with the aim of being confirmed in his righteousness, the other so that he may at least find mercy for his sins. Both subject themselves to the same standard.

We, too, came to church this morning 'to pray', if presenting oneself to God and uttering what weighs on one's mind is praying. We too are seeking assurance about ourselves and about other people before the God who is supposed to be our mainstay and provide us with a firm orientation. We too are hungering for recognition; for without recognition no one can live. We too are seeking mercy in the things about ourselves which neither we nor anyone else can describe as good. If we are willing, let us in the Spirit this morning put ourselves alongside those two kinds of people in the parable, and see what we can discover from them about ourselves.

The drama begins:

Scene One   The Pharisee appears on the stage. We will stop calling him 'the Pharisee', because through long Christian tradition the Pharisee has become the villain, the bogey man. He has also unfortunately become the figure of odium in which Christian anti-Judaism is crystallized – Jew Süss, Shylock, the Pharisees, the Jews; and God has rejected them. So we shall simply call the Pharisee 'the good man'.

Well, the good man takes the stage and strikes a pose. With face uncovered, head held high and hands outspread, he utters his prayer of thanksgiving, the prayer of innocence itself. It sounds like the annual reports we are given to read at the end of the year. Or like an election speech. He presents himself, righteous and good as he is, and waits for the applause. The God whom he thanks is merely the heavenly echo of the human ego which displays itself here in all its glory. But what has the good man actually to offer?

What he offers is merely *a negative identity*, like so many political and ecclesiastical election candidates, with their vapid alternatives. 'I thank thee that I am not' like the others – the wicked, the unjust, the adulterers, or that repulsive tax collector over there in the corner. But what he is, actually and positively, he is unable to say. Neither God nor man could draw any positive conclusions from these negative premises. It is surely a scanty identity which is acquired by being able to say who one is not. Who am I? Well, I am certainly not an exploiter, but I am not a 'radical' either. Of course I am not a Marxist or Leninist – but needless to say I am not a police spy. Anyone who can only talk about himself like this has a totally aggressive identity. He has found no certainty in himself, and is evidently suffering from lack of personality; so his anxiety builds up negative figures of this kind, with the aim of tracing a demarcation line between himself and other people. Anyone who can only thank God for all the things he is not can talk a long time without ever arriving at his real self. He beats about the bush. He slinks round himself, trying to mark off his own limits. What he has to thank God for is really – nothing, nothing at all. Instead of being sorry for the unpleasant tax collector in the corner, he uses him, too, merely as a doormat, so that he can stand a little higher himself. He condemns 'the others' in himself. He condemns 'the others' in general, and the tax collector in particular, in order to set himself in the proper light.

How many people do this? How often do we do it? Why? Out of anxiety and inner insecurity. Really, the good man is lying. Who is most ready to judge and least prepared to save, like this man here? It is precisely the person who does not take the good seriously and who deceives God and himself. He condemns the wicked most severely and is incessantly prepared to condemn the godless. And the person he is really judging without realizing it is himself.

So with a negative personal identity one has not much to show for oneself, before God, oneself or other people.

The good man only arrives at something positive when he diverts attention from his person and points to his 'good works': he fasts twice a week and gives ten per cent of his income for the poor. Is that not something? That is worth talking about! We could all take a leaf out of his book. Fasting twice a week and giving ten per cent – that would level up conditions between the rich and poor nations in the world. Fasting twice a week and giving ten per cent – that could be the new life-style for authentic Christian living. Fasting twice and giving ten per cent – with that, deserts could be irrigated, slums cleared and poor nations developed. Fasting twice a week and giving ten per cent was the great theme of the Assembly of the World Council of Churches in Uppsala in 1968. Even though in the end the money was less than planned, there was still enough to build up Interchurch Aid, Overseas Aid and Bread for the World. So what more is needed? Another few per cent? Or is what is lacking something quite different? In 1975 a well-known European church leader came to the Assembly of the World Council of Churches in Nairobi armed with large donations of money. He invited the heads of the African churches to come and discuss how these gifts could best be distributed. They never appeared. Why not? They gave this as their reason: 'We don't want your money. We want you yourselves. We certainly need help, unfortunately. But we need brothers even more. Who are you?' they asked us.

So what is lacking in the twice-weekly fast and the ten per cent? It is the human person who opens himself and gives himself. What is lacking is humanity, brotherliness, solidarity and friendship. It is only these things that can prevent the receiver from feeling humiliated by the help he is given. So with positive attainments – fasting twice a week and giving ten per cent – we still have nothing to show for ourselves – nothing to show before God, other people or ourselves. The person who does a great deal, has a great deal and gives a great deal, but is nothing in himself is – yes, who is he really? A good person or a poor person? It seems to me that he is a dangerous person. People like that are not good to live among.

Scene Two   The tax collector enters. Again, we shall stop calling him 'the tax collector'. The long tradition of Christian sympathy has made this tax collector the prototype of the repentant sinner – the petty criminal who can be reformed, so to speak. Here we shall simply call him 'the bad man'. All his repentance cannot ultimately blind us to the fact that the man is corrupt through and through. Sympathy is completely out of place.

So the bad man comes on stage. But we can hardly see him. He stands to one side and 'far off', as our Bible translates it. He does not venture out into the floodlights where the good man stands, but stays in the twilight, the shadows. And that is the proper place for him.

He does not venture to look up to the Holy of Holies. Nor has he any reason to do so. He does not thank God with open hands. And they are certainly too dirty. He beats his breast. A pity he did not beat it harder still. He cries: 'God be merciful to me a sinner.' And in saying that he is at last uttering the complete truth about himself. For he is 'a sinner' – a bad man: before God, before the Law, before the standards of his own people, and before himself. If anyone can still be merciful to him, it can only be God.

What has the bad man to offer? No fasts and no ten per cent – or if ten per cent, then probably ten per cent in tax evasion. So he does not even begin to render an account of himself. This bad man accepts everything he has done, fully and completely, without beating about the bush. He takes everything on himself and acknowledges what he is to his own self: 'I, sinner.' In saying this he strips himself naked. There is nothing else he can do. And yet just by doing this, he *himself* is left. For in this very way the tax collector arrives at the truth about himself, as the sinner he is. It is a bitter truth. It is a truth destructive of all respect – a truth that might well be called suicidal. For a sinner has forfeited his rights. He no longer has any supporters. No one can save him. But it is *his* truth, it is he himself, his dignity in all his shame. And so God arrives at his rights. By giving judgment for God and not himself, he throws himself entirely on God's mercy. With this he reminds God and himself that the outskirts of the law are kindly: 'The Lord gives grace to the humble', we read in Prov. 3.34.

What has the bad man to offer? *Himself*. Nothing else? No, nothing else. He has nothing. He can do nothing. But he is here. He is this sinner. He finds room *in his own person* for everything he has done wrong: 'I, sinner.' And with this, corrupt though he is, he acquires a positive, personal identity. He does not blacken other people in order to set off his own virtues. He immediately begins to talk about himself. 'God be merciful to me a sinner.' A person who talks like this is an honest person. We know where we are with him. The bad man is not a dangerous person. One can live among 'sinners' like this.

Scene Three   We have now been to the temple, first with the good man and then with the bad man. We have talked first to the one and then to the other. That was not quite right, because the men are in the temple *at the same time*. They are dependent on one another. If we simply look at them individually, we spoil the parable. For really the Pharisee and the tax collector are the two opposite extremes of one and the same society. The Pharisee, as his name tells us, is someone apart only because of his aloofness from everything that makes him impure – which means from impure sinners and tax collectors as well. He becomes someone special only through his condemnation of other people who are not as he is. So he needs these 'others', and ultimately the tax collector too. Without them he would not be what he purports to be. The tax collector is in a similar position, but in reverse. For he would not feel like a sinner if it were not for these 'special people' who in comparable situations simply do not prove to be corruptible. If it were not for the Pharisee, the tax collector would only be doing 'what everyone else does', people who 'after all are no better than us', as we say. Leonhard Ragaz perceived a truth when he said about this parable: 'The Pharisee is to blame for the tax collector: he pushed him into the religious and social bondage in which the law ceased to matter to him any more' (*Die Gleichnisse Jesu. Seine soziale Botschaft*, Stundenbücher 99, 1971, p. 112). Of course the Pharisee is not to blame for the tax collector's tax evasions, but it is true that he turns him into the sinner, the outcast, the man with a stigma. Through his public condemnation he pins the tax collector down, and takes away his every hope.

In almost every group, whether in the church or society as a whole, there are the 'high fliers' who dominate everything – the top of the class, the leaders, the people who decide what is good and what is bad. And then there are the people at the bottom of the ladder – 'the dregs,' which the group or society uses as a way of acquiring a profile for itself, because they embody everything that is 'wicked'. Pharisees and tax collectors are the exponents of a social gulf, the gulf between 'the good and the bad', 'the just and the unjust', 'God's children' and 'people who hate God', 'believers' and 'unbelievers'. Whenever this gulf is fixed, a merciless struggle begins – the struggle between the supposedly 'good' people and the allegedly 'bad' ones. Because in this struggle everyone is either a friend or an enemy, it is bound to end with the apocalyptic extermination of the allegedly 'bad' people. How does this conflict arise? It has its genesis in the social gulf which the parable stylizes through the Pharisee and the tax collector. And how does the gulf arise? It has its genesis in 'the good man'. He claims the good as his own property and presents it as just that. All possession is dangerous because it brings anxiety with it. But the possession of the good is the most appalling danger of all, because it rips open the gap between the good and the bad. Because there are no steps leading from one side of the gap to the other, the conflict ends in the single alternative: life or death. Whenever industrial struggles, or struggles for property and social power, or differences of belief in the church, are bound up with this gulf between good and bad – and when are they not? – hell is let loose, unfortunately in the quite literal sense. Every socialist molehill then turns into an apocalyptic mountain.

Every deviating opinion seems then to be accompanied by the smell of brimstone.

Do not let us deceive ourselves, here in this church either. We may be sitting quite amiably next to one another; but this frightful struggle between 'the good people' and 'the bad ones' is latent in us, too, and can break out at any moment.

Scene Four. Finale The person telling the parable enters the stage and pronounces sentence. Jesus introduces his judgment with weighty solemnity: 'But I tell you. . .' Here Jesus is speaking in the name of God himself. This is a shock that shatters even the language of the parable. In the first place, no one can know what two people prayed in the temple except the God to whom they prayed. Secondly, Jesus' 'I tell you' follows directly on the tax collector's cry, 'God be merciful to me a sinner'. It is the divine 'I' which Jesus uses and which utters itself through his words. And what does this divine judgment say?

It declares the tax collector and sinner to be righteous 'rather than' the just Pharisee. 'This man went down to his house justified rather than the other.' Some manuscripts leave out 'rather than the other' altogether. Then the pronouncement sounds harsher still. The tax collector went down to his house justified. The Pharisee is not even worth talking about any more. What does this mean?

Jesus declares that in God's eyes right is on the side of the tax collector, not the Pharisee. Jesus declares that the tax collector is not merely granted the grace he prayed for. 'God be *merciful* to me a sinner' was what he asked for. 'He went down to his house *justified*' – that is the response. The answer is far greater than the request. If Jesus had only wanted to say how inconceivably good God can be, then he would merely have had to say: the Pharisee went to his house justified, and God had mercy on the tax collector. Then each of them would have received his due, and Jesus would have been as 'well-balanced' as we are always being told to be today. And everyone would have been quite content – including ourselves.

But the radical from Nazareth turns everything upside down: the sinner goes home justified, while to the righteous man God is not even gracious. This is hard for all the 'good' people – and extremely surprising for the 'bad' ones. If we appeal to the importance of good and bad in the social order, we might even say that it menaces society.

If we look at the Pharisee and the tax collector, each for himself, as individuals, then Jesus' judgment really is incomprehensible, and indeed unjust. But when we perceive the devilish gulf which the Pharisee opens up between himself and the tax collector, when he seizes the good for himself and pushes the other man into evil, then Jesus' judgment about justification becomes a liberating judgment – for the tax collector first of all, and then really for the Pharisee too. Ultimately it is not these individual people who are in question, but the vicious circle in which the one person becomes guilty because of the way he judges the other, and in which social and psychological death are disseminated through self-righteousness and the condemnation of others.

We will only be liberated from this vicious circle when we face ourselves and God with the judgment of Jesus and the tax collector's confession. And we all – I too – belong to the 'certain people' who, when it comes to the point, exalt themselves by disparaging others. And with this we lose sight of ourselves and God and other people.

Jesus' justifying judgment brings about a splendid inward and outward deliverance. God condemns the good person who I want to be, but am not; and accepts the bad person who I do not want to be, but am.

In community with Jesus, people have continually discovered that God accepts our tax collector's soul and rejects our Pharisee's soul. In community with Jesus, 'the friend of sinners and tax collectors', we see that we are loved – and how much we are loved – in the place where we do not want to be at all: in community with the people we despise. In community with Jesus, we discover that doors open – the door to the repressed self in our inmost heart, and the door to the repressed 'other' who is at our side.

'God be merciful to me a sinner.' That is the truth, the whole truth and nothing but the truth in us. No one can go beyond this. Happy is the person who enters into it, rests in it, and continually returns to it. 'We are beggars, that's the truth,' as Luther put it.

'This man went down to his house justified.' That is the still greater truth of God about us. This is Jesus for us, Jesus beside us and Jesus with us. Happy is the person who lives in this assurance. For 'if God be for us, who can be against us?'

Before the sermon we listened to what is sometimes called the Pharisee's psalm, Psalm 26. In the spirit of what we have heard, let us now pray 'the tax collector's psalm', Psalm 51, so that we may learn who we in truth are, 'beloved sinners', and may go to our homes justified.

Prayer
Have mercy on me, O God, according to thy steadfast love; according to thy abundant mercy blot out my transgressions. Wash me thoroughly from my iniquity, and cleanse me from my sin. For I know my transgressions, and my sin is ever before me. Against thee, thee only, have I sinned, and done that which is evil in thy sight, so that thou art justified in thy sentence and blameless in thy judgment... Behold, thou desirest truth in the inward being; therefore teach me wisdom in my secret heart... Create in me a clean heart, O God, and put a new and right spirit within me. Cast me not away from thy presence, and take not thy holy spirit from me. Restore to me the joy of thy salvation, and uphold me with a joyful spirit...

12 Accept One Another

Accept one another, therefore, as Christ has accepted you for the glory of God. . . And may the God of hope fill you with all joy and peace in believing, so that you may abound in hope more and more through the power of the Holy Spirit (Rom. 15.7,13).

I should like to preach so that instead of being many separate listeners we may become one congregation. I should like to speak so that individuals and individualists may be fused into a community in which one person looks at another and acknowledges him and accepts him. But this cannot be done by talking – or not, at any rate, if only one person is speaking. Acceptance requires two people at least. Their talking and listening must be reciprocal. How can that happen in this church? How can it be made possible through this service?

When other people look at us with friendly eyes, we come alive. When other people recognize us for the individuals we are, we become free. And when we feel accepted and affirmed, we are happy. For human beings depend on acceptance as birds depend on the air, and fish on water. Acceptance is humanity's element. If acceptance is lacking, the air becomes thin, we cannot breathe properly, and shrivel up. That is why we shrink back under an indifferent glance, are wounded by disregard, and perish as human beings if we are rejected. It is easy for us to accept one another when other people are like ourselves. But if they are different from us, we find it difficult.

'Accept one another.' When Paul wrote these words he was

thinking about the Christian community in Rome. It was made up of Jews and Gentiles. The Jewish Christians were already in a minority, and it was through Gentile Christians that the church was growing. But the Jewish Christians felt that they were the true believers, the elder brothers. Did they accept the Gentiles only as 'second-class Christians'? At all events Paul, the Jewish Christian, explains to his blood brothers here: God's acceptance of us in Christ is shown by the fact that he has mercy on the Gentiles. The hope which fills us is not a Jewish privilege. It is grace that is available for everyone, without any presuppositions or any conditions.

Gentile Christianity is certainly not our problem now, as it was for the Jews then; and if Paul were to talk to us today, he would probably have to say exactly the reverse. In his own time he was trying to build up a community of Jews and Gentiles. But we Gentile Christians have to try to achieve a community of Gentiles and Jews, if we want to arrive at the same objective. And this brings us up against the limits of what we are prepared to accept. Christian and political antisemitism have in the past portrayed the Jew as the scum of creation. It began with the boycott, 'A German does not buy from Jews.' This was followed by the accusation, 'It's all the Jews' fault.' It ended with Auschwitz. And we know where that led the Jews – and us. The person who is not accepted is soon driven out and exterminated. Unfortunately this is not merely something belonging to the far-away past. The appalling UNO resolution of 1975, denouncing Zionism as a form of racism, is a sign that Auschwitz can be repeated on a world-wide scale. Whatever political solution is found in the Middle East, solidarity between Christians and Jews is now of supreme urgency. If today the Jews suffer and are isolated, Christians will suffer and be isolated too – or if not they will be guilty. Shall we find the courage to accept the Jews, courage for solidarity with Israel? Or are these merely pious words which will fade away at the next oil crisis?

Accept one another: there are people among us who are 'always welcome', as we say. Others are merely 'put up with'. Our society belongs to the healthy and the efficient; so the people who are only 'put up with' are the people who are handicapped, either mentally or physically. Their lot with us even now must still be described as the fate of being merely put up with. Our defensive reactions handicap them even more; and the social consequences of being handicapped are often worse than the handicap itself. Why is this so?

Evidently the non-handicapped person is at first frightened when he meets someone with a handicap. He feels disconcerted. He finds it difficult to see his handicapped counterpart as a human being. He first of all sees only the deformity, and is upset by it. For the person he wants to meet in this encounter is himself. This defensive reaction turns the handicapped person into a kind of leper – isolated, ignored, or made miserable by pity. The handicapped are not our problem. We are theirs. It is only when the non-handicapped cease to be a problem for the handicapped that the practical problems can be solved too. Where shall we find the strength for the acceptance and community that is required here?

Accept one another: lack of relationship is ultimately our affliction in the church too – in our service this morning as well. 'When my wife and I moved to K. three years ago,' someone wrote to me, 'we felt the need to make contact with our local church. We hoped to make new friends. When we went to church we heard good sermons, on which the minister had expended a great deal of time and trouble, and which gave us something to think about. But our hope that we would make real contact with our fellow Christians in the same pew came to nothing. We left church as solitary as we were when we entered it.' Is this supposed to be all that congregational life is about? Can this be called a living church? Of course we can join special groups. But even then, contacts often end when we shut our front door behind us. Can things go on like this? A preaching church in which we receive something, without a community in which we give something?

What is the reason for this reserve under which we let other people suffer and then ultimately suffer ourselves?

It is probably that we accept other people, even those closest to us, only in the guise of our own picture of them, and only in the light of our own prejudices. In that case, we are not seeking the other person at all, but only ourselves in the other person. We leave him alone, and remain alone ourselves. Another reason is probably that we only accept one another on a mutual basis: 'tit for tat' There is an ancient principle for human relationships. According to Aristotle, it is 'like draws to like'. This kind of sociality certainly fuses people together, but only people of the same kind: white people with white, Christians with Christians, the healthy with the healthy, students with students, professors with their colleagues, and so on. This seems the most natural thing in the world for the people who are 'in'. But 'the outsiders' feel hurt. We prefer to 'keep ourselves to ourselves', and accordingly stew in our own juice.

Birds of a feather flock together. Why, in fact? Well, people who are like ourselves, who think the same, have the same, and want the same, corroborate us. But people who are different from us, who think and feel differently, or want different things, make us unsure of ourselves. That is why we love people who are like ourselves and avoid people who are different. And when these 'different' people live among us, need attention, and require interest and humanity from us, we react defensively, with exaggerated self-assertion, anxiety and disparagement. This is in fact the root of racism, antisemitism, the handicapping of the handicapped and – not least – lack of human contacts in the church. 'Birds of a feather flock together' is nothing other than the social form adopted by self-righteousness. It is an expression of fear. That is why this form of self-righteousness always involves aggression towards the people who cause the insecurity. It has no confidence and no self-confidence.

Accept one another: as we have seen, this unfortunately has its limits. 'Accept one another *as Christ has accepted you.*' It is only this that gives us a new direction. It is only this that breaks through our limitations, so that we can do what seems to be contrary to the gloomy introversion of our natures. This makes us receptive for the other person as he is, so that we can enjoy him and be interested in him.

So now let us try to forget ourselves, and simply ask how and in what way Christ has accepted us.

To put it simply, God suffers from us because he loves us. Love and suffering go together. He suffers us gladly. Can we suffer other people? Can other people endure us? Can we endure ourselves? Who are all the people 'we can't stand'? We continually make one another suffer – brothers and sisters, man and wife, parents and children, neighbours and the people we work with. These same stones send out ripples into the church and political life too. If we cannot endure each other, then we will not put up with anything either. But if we can endure one another, then we do not take things amiss. Christ reveals to us God's love, with its endless capacity for endurance, for suffering. His love is passion – passion for men and women and their dignity, passion for creation and its peace. Because of his infinite passion, God takes upon himself the passion and death of Christ, so that we may become free and can live together for his glory. Through his suffering from us and his death for us, Christ has accepted us and brought us to be God's glory. We have to sink ourselves deeply into the passion of Christ again if we are to perceive this: he suffers from us because he suffers us so gladly – which is to say because he loves us. The extent of his passion for us is revealed through the depths of the passion he himself endured. When we discern the suffering his passion for us endured, and endures still, then we are disarmed. We become free of our tense self-endorsement. We stop being frightened for ourselves. We become receptive for other people. Prejudices fall like scales from our eyes. We become attentive, interested, enter into others and give of ourselves. Other people no longer make us feel insecure, because we no longer need to affirm ourselves. Just because he is different, the other person becomes a surprise which we gladly accept. We can accept ourselves because Christ has accepted us for God's glory. Because he has already accepted other people, and accepts us, the whole landscape of life opens up before us in an endless vista. So where we accept one another, recognize one another and affirm one another, we are on firm ground. We cannot go far enough. In the light of the life which God passionately affirms and accepts, no life is without value and no life is 'second-class'. The suffering of his love has transformed everything, and the more we go out of ourselves, the more we discover this and experience it.

A few lines before our text, Paul says the same thing more trenchantly. 'Christ did not live to please himself but, as it is written, "the reproaches of those who reproached thee fell on me".' Anyone who does not live to please himself – which involves remaining alone – but lives to please others, can endure these reproaches. But Paul's sentence pierces deeply into our ideas of glory and ignominy. We are no longer 'reproached' by God, but are brought to glory through the reproaches which Christ endured. Nor are we alone in the struggle for glory and repute. The wounds that wound us have fallen on him. So we no longer have laboriously to save our faces. We can put up with slander and mistrust, because these have already been borne – even borne away – by him. So we do not need to reproach others, so as to put ourselves in the right. There is a hymn that used once to be sung more often than it is today:

Jesus, thy blood and righteousness
My beauty is, my glorious dress;
Midst flaming world, in this arrayed,
with joy shall I lift up my head.

If Christ's 'blood and righteousness' is to be our support before God and in eternity, how much more must this be true before human beings and in time! This faith is a 'beauty' and a 'glory' that is irreplaceable and which no one but our own fear can rob us of.

If God loves us so much that he is prepared to suffer for us, and from us and with us, then we too shall at last be free – free for transformation. We don't have to hold fast to our image of ourselves or our own reputation. For we ourselves are held fast and can no longer be lost. So we can unfold, and change.

No one has to nail a person down to his deeds or misdeeds. We can endure the other person and go with him, without imposing our own picture and preconception of him. God's liberty and future have been thrown wide open to us in the community of Christ, so we can liberate one another and hold the future open for one another. Because, as Jesus has shown, God has pleasure in us, he is pleased to put up with a great deal from us, as we wander and stray through life. The same is true of our own community together. We are pleased to put up with differences, conflicts and criticism because we have found lasting pleasure in one another. If we were not acknowledged by Christ and brought to God's glory, accepted with all our unpleasant crotchets and rough edges and passionately loved – if it were not for this, who should we be? A dead leaf blowing in the wind, a speck of dust on the road. But if this passionate divine acceptance is true – and I believe it is more certain than we often think – who are we then?

Then we are no longer solitary individualists. We are a community in which one person accepts the other in the same way that Christ accepts us. Then the dreary old principle that 'birds of a feather flock together' no longer applies. Now people who are different accept one another and find pleasure in one another. Then Christian fellowship – which means liberating fellowship – no longer means just sitting down beside the people I agree with. It means sitting beside the people I don't agree with – and staying there. Then we will stop meeting just to corroborate one another by way of the same old stories, jokes and judgments about other people. Then we create an open community, a hospitable community, and bring friendliness into the unfriendly corners of this society of ours.

The Christian community or congregation then ceases to be simply the sum total of the people in the parish register or on the church's membership roll. It is then a new kind of living together. It means:

that no one is left alone with his problems;

that no one has to conceal his handicaps;

that there is no one group of people who have the say about what is to be done, and another group who have no say;

that neither old people nor children are isolated;

that one person bears with the other, even if it is difficult and even when there is disagreement between them;

that one person can leave another person in peace, if peace is what he needs.

Does this open community of acceptance exist? We should be badly off if it were merely a demand confronting us, a demand made by the Bible. But if we open our eyes we can discover this community even among ourselves. He who seeks, finds.

In the midst of our 'preaching' churches without community, groups are growing up everywhere which are prepared to exchange 'private' life for the life of community, opening their homes to make this possible. Basic communities and integrated congregations can be found. One only has to look round a little. Remedies for the sickness of private, non-committal Christianity exist. Communities of this kind are of a manageable size, for if people do not know one another, they cannot accept one another. They are open, so that lonely people can come in. For many people, they heal the sufferings society has inflicted on them. They are communities which eat and drink with open doors, so that anyone can join in. They are voluntary communities, open for personal initiative.

I do not believe that the lack of human contacts in our churches can be overcome except through the building up of community churches from below. Whereas in our preaching churches 'the fellowship of the table' is notoriously lacking, these communities gather round the table of the Lord. To the service of worship they add the common feast.

It is regrettably true that society and the church often refuse to accept these communities, and plague them with mistrust. If a student looks for a room by himself it is hard enough. But if a group of students looks for somewhere to live, they generally meet with refusal. And when these community groups even go so far as to undertake certain tasks on behalf of people living on the fringes of our society – if they live and work with the handicapped, discharged prisoners, drug addicts or political outcasts – then they are viewed in an increasingly dubious light. In this town and its environs there have already been citizen action groups to protest against experiments of this kind. Anyone who eats with 'tax collectors and sinners' is easily compromised and denounced for being 'the friend of tax collectors and sinners'. Anyone who exerts himself on behalf of the rejected often meets with more rejection than help himself. In the church at least, let us put an end to the discrimination against student communities, experiments in communal living and group initiatives for social action. Then we should have made a start with the acceptance of the non-accepted. There has to be advice and criticism where it is called for, but it must not turn into rejection and the withdrawal of the rights of other people to live, and to live as they feel called to do.

But we do not *only* find that handicapped people are handicapped still more by the rest of us. There are also communities made up of the healthy and the handicapped, which give people the courage to live. By this I do not mean 'aid for the handicapped' schemes, but communities in which handicapped people live together with their non-handicapped fellows. Anyone who has a genuine interest in projects of this kind can easily discover the relevant addresses and seek them out at any time. It is not impossible to overcome the vicious circle of mutual anxiety and fear. It can disappear like a bad dream, when the people who feel insecure are shown, by word and example, practicable ways of community and acceptance. Let me give an example. Last summer twenty physically handicapped and twenty non-handicapped people travelled to Langeoog, one of the North Sea islands, to spend a holiday together. The project was arranged by a Protestant youth organization. The group was determined to demonstrate on the promenade, if necessary, in order to show that here were people who had as much right to bathe on the beach as the rest of the sun-tanned holiday-makers. The demonstration was unnecessary. The way the group bathed, played and danced together, with their wheelchairs, was so infectious that other holiday-makers joined in spontaneously. An exception? Of course. But it shows what can be done.

A person who has withdrawn into himself has no hope. He is frightened. A closed society has no future. It kills the hope of people on the fringe, and ultimately atrophies of its own accord. Hope is lived where we come out of our shells and participate in the life of others, in both joy and pain. Hope assumes concrete form in open community with other people. God has accepted us and has hope for us. This keeps us alive and gives us the courage to be, in spite of all attempts at intimidation. So let us accept one another without prejudice. Let us hope for one another, so that we too may sustain one another in life and give each other the courage for a living humanity.

May the God of hope fill you with all joy and peace in believing: you who go out to meet one another; you who accept one another and have pleasure in one another; you who pay the price of your own rejection, so as to accept the rejected. Become richer in hope through the power of the Spirit, you who live with the handicapped, discharged prisoners or drug addicts, and who bring fellowship into the abandoned corners of our society. This is not merely a pious wish with no force behind it. It is a real experience. Hope is given us for the sake of the hopeless, and in community with them our hope becomes certainty. We are accepted in Christ so that we may accept other people; and the more resolutely we accept other people, the more certain we shall be of our own acceptance in him.

13 Solidarity

This morning I should like us to think about a concept which does not spring from the language of the Bible and is not moulded by Christian theology. Solidarity is the key word of the international labour movement, and the basic value it acknowledges. Solidarity is the profoundest theme of Marxist socialism, religious socialism and, today, of authentic socialism too, when workers rebel against party dictatorship as they are doing in Poland. Solidarity is a sacred word for every socialist. It means standing shoulder to shoulder, struggling together, suffering for one another and living with one another in a single community. Christians have certainly no right to appropriate this concept and to adopt it for themselves. Socialist solidarity deserves the greatest respect. It must not be pocketed by the church. But it will be permissible for us to ask a few questions which are of relevance to ourselves.

Is solidarity – the word and the concept – another expression for the Christian way of life too, and for the motives behind Christian action? Is neighbourly love the Christian term for solidarity? Is solidarity the socialist word for neighbourly love? How can neighbourly love and solidarity be critically related to one another, and how do they complement one another? What can Christians and socialists learn from one another?

Solidarity means struggling together

The proletariat had to stand shoulder to shoulder and to struggle together in order to defend themselves against capitalist rule and exploitation. Only the solidarity of the whole working class was able to stand up to the class struggle imposed from above.

Class struggle imposed from above means *divide et impera* – divide and rule, rule by means of division. If people are isolated from one another, divided, separated, and then treated and paid differently, then one group of workers can always be stirred up and set against the others: white-collar workers against labour, immigrant workers against the native ones, men against women, the unemployed against people with jobs, countries with sweated labour against the industrial countries, and so on. Fear of losing their jobs, and therefore their living, isolates people. Everyone becomes his own best friend. Aggression is generated, not against the employer, but against competitors in the struggle for wages, and against the people pushing up from behind in the struggle for work. Then the oppressed begin to oppress one another. The tormented begin to torment themselves. Their sense of impotence causes a backlash on people who are weaker still. It strikes inwards and becomes a rage that consumes the person himself. The results are apathy and alcoholism. And this is how the rule of the few over the many works. Divide and rule. Control becomes total. The mechanism of fear comes into play.

The struggle for liberty from below is directed against this class struggle imposed from above. The helpless have only one strength: their solidarity. Individuals can do nothing. But *together* they build a counter-force, and *in solidarity* with one another they become unconquerable. Class rule retreats before the collective and united solidarity of the working class. The solidarity of the working class frightens even party dictatorship, as we can see at the moment in Poland. 'The people at the top' can do what they like with isolated individuals, people who are divided from one another. But together we can resist. We learnt that in the citizen action groups. When everyone only looks at himself we are afraid. But hope springs up in the community of solidarity. That is a very simple truth. Everyone can understand it. So why do we continually forget it? Why do we allow ourselves to be so easily corrupted? Martin Niemöller once described this process very simply and honestly, and we have all gone through similar experiences ourselves:

> When the Communists were taken away in 1933, I held my tongue and did nothing about it. After all, I wasn't a Communist.
> When they took away the Social Democrats I held my tongue and did nothing about it. After all, I wasn't a Social Democrat.
> When after that they took away the Jews and murdered them, I held my tongue and did nothing about it. After all, I wasn't a Jew.

When they finally took me away and put me in a concentration camp there was no one left who could have cried out on my behalf or done anything for me.

The hope of being able to save oneself by surrendering other people and leaving them in the lurch is a false delusion. Our egoism makes us weaker and weaker. There is only one way of protecting every single one of us: solidarity with the first victims, solidarity with the weakest among us. What affects them today will affect us tomorrow. So their skins are our own.

Anyone who puts himself on the side of the handicapped in our society is defending his own health. Anyone who puts himself on the side of the oppressed in El Salvador is defending his own liberty. Anyone who resists the isolation of his opponent is acting out of love for his own life.

Solidarity is the brotherhood-in-arms of the oppressed

Christians can learn from this that this brotherhood-in-arms among the oppressed is neighbourly love in situations of crisis. For in a political context the commandment about neighbourly love means resisting tyranny, liberating the oppressed and promoting the equal rights of everyone.

Solidarity means compassion, suffering with others, bearing our burdens together

It is not merely political oppression and economic exploitation that ruin people. Suffering, guilt, fear and grief destroy us too, because they isolate us. So nothing is more important than to find people who stand by us in trouble, and stay beside us, and bear our burdens with us. 'A friend in need is a friend indeed' the proverb tells us. And 'a trouble shared is a trouble halved'. Of course this cannot mean that the whole sum of suffering can be distributed, or that the degree of pain is thereby diminished. But the suffering *in* suffering – the loneliness and the forsakenness – can be ended through solidarity in the depths. We need the fellowship of other people at the very point where neither we ourselves nor anyone else can help us. We need trust at the very point where we can do nothing more. But it is just at the frontier where no one can help us and no one can do anything that solidarity generally stops. 'Sincere sympathy', we say. And, 'Can

I do anything for you?' But when there is nothing more to be done and there is no more help for us, then one person after another goes away; and this is the point when we too forsake the others. Why? Because we think that practical help – the deed, the action – is the only answer we have to give to suffering, pain and fear. But compassion, sharing another person's guilt, grieving with him and standing by him when he is dying, demands a solidarity that goes beyond activism and the illusion that there is something to be *done* about everything. It demands a fellowship in impotence, in helplessness, and even in silence. This is what I would call community in the depths. It has become something alien for modern men and women. They find it deeply repellent, because it is in such crass contradiction to their 'active' attitude to living. It makes them feel insecure and called in question. Anyone who responds to pain merely with activity, to suffering simply with offers of help, and to grief with attempts at distraction, knows nothing about this solidarity in the depths. He is only trying to compensate for the suffering, and his readiness to help merely increases the loneliness of the victim.

It is only the person who knows loneliness and does not flee from it who can hold community with the lonely. It is only the person who knows the frontier where all human help fails who can stand by the helpless. It is only the person who knows the guilt which no one can make good who can remain beside the guilty. It is only the person who has made dying a part of his life and no longer represses it who can accompany the dying.

Solidarity in the depths is the community of the suffering, the guilty and those who mourn. They can no longer help themselves, and support one another simply through that very fact. I believe that no fellowship is more profound and no sympathy communicates a deeper happiness than this solidarity in the depths.

Solidarity means living in community

Who is prepared to live in community with whom? That is the question. The fundamental law of all natural communities is 'birds of a feather flock together'. That is why 'dog doesn't eat dog'. We find homogeneous communities of this kind everywhere: the same class, the same race, the same religion, the same language, the same interests bind people together. These are the 'dog doesn't eat dog' communities. They are more than merely pragmatic in purpose, because the person who is like ourselves corroborates us, while anyone who is different makes us insecure and fearful. That is why we love people like ourselves and hate people who are different. We need people who share our opinions and are on our own wavelength, to satisfy our insatiable hunger for self-corroboration. So the homogeneous community is not really a natural community at all. It is a community for the common suppression of fear through permanent self-corroboration – which means that it is a highly *un*natural community.

In societies which become pluralistic for one reason or another – in which people of different classes, races and religions have to put up with one another – the uniformity principle leads to segregation, to apartheid; white people draw to white people, black people to black, Christians to Christians, atheists to atheists, the healthy to the healthy, the handicapped to the handicapped, the successful to the successful, the old to the old, and so on.

Here everyone finds a place in his own group, and every group stews in its own juice. Life in our own group certainly covers up our fear, but it leads to the impoverishment of life and to the boredom that reduces people to idiocy. Everywhere we meet the same people, talk the same language, laugh dutifully at the same jokes.

But the Christian principle of community is the messianic principle, which means it is *the principle of hope*. Here people who are dissimilar are united, develop a vital interest in one another and become similar through their creative love.

This is what we see in Jesus, who came to seek the lost, to accept the sinners who had been cast out of society, and to heal lepers. This is what we experience in his community. It is no longer a matter of: here Jew, there Gentile; here the educated, there the uneducated; here the master, there the servant; here the man, there the woman. No, they all become one in Jesus the Messiah and joint-heirs of the promise of the divine future (cf. Gal. 3.28f.).

Bound together through the power of reconciliation, the barriers which people have erected in front of themselves out of fear, fall. The common hope creates the same rights for everyone. So here solidarity becomes *creative*. It does not merely bind together people who are in any case similar, but makes the unlike like in the new community of the future.

Solidarity as a common struggle unites people who are alike in being oppressed. Solidarity as community in the depths unites people who are alike in their suffering. But solidarity in hopeful love goes beyond these limits. Where it exists it turns the unloved into people who are beloved, the repressed into interesting partners, and disagreeable enemies into the loveliest of friends.

The solidarity of hopeful love breaks through the principle of similarity by recognizing the other person in his differences. It is only this recognition of the other which takes a person beyond his own group. Through this recognition we discover vital interest in people who are different from ourselves: non-handicapped in the handicapped, people of one race or colour or nationality in people of another race or colour or nationality. It is not hopeful and creative community if I sit beside someone with whom I agree in any case, but only if I sit next to someone I do not agree with, and stay there.

The solidarity of creative love heals the wounds of a segregated society. This is the source of communities that heal. And they find their foundation and their continually new encouragement when they look at Jesus the Messiah, of whom Paul said: 'Accept one another as Christ has accepted you, for the glory of God the Father.'

This is the divine solidarity in which we live, and from which we live, and which surrounds us with sympathy that is without limits or boundaries, so that we may open ourselves for one another and

struggle together,
share one another's burdens,
and learn to live in fellowship and community with one another.

14 Good Friday: The Birth of Hope from the Cross of Christ

Ave crux – unica spes, we can sometimes read in old churchyards: Hail cross, our only hope! If one takes the phrase seriously it sounds so nonsensical as to be embarrassing. For hope surely means life and love. Hope is on the look-out for happiness and success. And whatever we think of when we consider the cross, it undoubtedly means the end: a disappointed hope, a betrayed love, a tortured body and a godforsaken death. What has hope to do with the cross? What business has the spring of life with so bitter an end? How can a death become the foundation for a unique hope for living?

While there's life there's hope. That is true. We hope as long as we live, and we are alive and wide-awake as long as we can still hope. When we hope, we open ourselves for the future. Our senses become alert. Our hearts expand and are receptive for what is to come. Hope makes us capable of experiencing happiness, for hope is in love with success, not failure.

But hope also makes us deeply vulnerable to the pain of disappointment. Only hope can be disappointed. Hope makes life vital and lovely. But hope also makes death deadly, and turns dumb suffering into conscious pain.

So we are taking a risk if we make hope the direction in which we live. That is why we really only hope, and unfold through hope, to the extent to which we can trust. Without trust in the kindness of fate we would not open ourselves for what is to come. We would close up apprehensively and defend ourself against the continual uncertainties of the future. Without trust we can dare nothing, and win nothing either. Hope, opening ourselves for experience, and a surplus of trust, make life worth living, because they make it worth loving. But where do we find a trust which not only makes us capable of happiness but also makes us ready to endure pain? Who gives us a confidence which sustains not only our living but our dying too?

If living means hoping, then the opposite is true as well: the person who loses hope in life dies. Can hope be disappointed? asked Ernst Bloch. And he answered: Yes, it can; but this painful experience is open to hope alone. The person who hopes for nothing cannot be disappointed either. But is he still a living person? He is more like a corpse. Every disappointment leads to numbness, to petrifaction. We are petrified with horror. We are paralysed. We are speechless. And this numbness of the heart is the beginning of dying. For to die means to become numb and cold. A great life-work is abruptly broken off through incurable illness; we are numb. A love that made one happy is wounded to death, through another's guilt. We grow hard. A hopeful youth is handicapped, humiliated and intimidated through prohibitions. The boy or girl becomes bitter and cynical. So many of our life stories are marked by disappointed hopes. And the odour of *rigor mortis* can be sensed in many an encounter with living people.

So hoping is a fool's game, we are told, for hope is always disappointed and 'hope deferred makes the heart sick'. Experience makes us wise, not hope. How much petrified life, how much life that has been fooled by hope – which means how much dead life – is to be found within us and round about us! One might just as well say that life means burying hopes, taking punishment, swallowing disappointments, doing without, forgetting.

So the real question that concerns us is not, can hope be disappointed? It is, how can hope surmount its disappointments without surrendering? Can a hope exempt from crises emerge from the crises of hope we endure? Or, to put the question in very simple terms: can hope be born again?

The cross – our only hope, says the Christian faith. What has hope to do with death? What has the passion for life to do with that ugly gibbet with its endless prolongation of the death-agony?

The centre of the Christian faith is a history: the history of the living and dying, death and resurrection of Christ. I do not merely want to *discuss* the utility or the disadvantage of hope in life, either with the happily hopeful among us or with the disappointed, either with those of us who are confident or with those who feel betrayed. What I should like to do is to narrate this history. I should like to be able to tell it in such a way that we rediscover ourselves in it, so that out of it our hope may be born again.

At the centre of the Christian faith is a history – the history of Christ's passion. We have to take this quite literally, which is to say in the double sense of the word 'passion'. The history of Christ is the history of a great passion, a passionate hope. For that very reason it is also the history of an unheard-of suffering, a deathly agony.

At the centre of the Christian faith is the suffering of the passionate Christ. The story of the passion has this active and this passive side. In earlier times people often overlooked the *passion* of Christ which led him into suffering. The man of sorrows then became the prototype of dumb submission to a painful fate; for passion counted as sin, and only patience was a virtue.

Nowadays people like to overlook the *suffering* that is part of every great passion. People want to be perfectly happy, so they suppress suffering. They stifle pain, and rob themselves of feeling at the same time. Life without passion is poverty-stricken. Life without the readiness for suffering is shallow. We have to overcome both our fear of passion and our fear of suffering. Otherwise hope cannot be born again.

Let us pause at two stations of Christ's passion, and ask what happened there: Gethsemane and Golgotha.

The story of the passion did not only begin when Christ was taken prisoner and tortured by the Roman soldiers. It started much earlier, really already in the province of Galilee, at the moment when Christ decided to go to Jerusalem with his disciples, to the centre of power. For it was in Jerusalem that his passion for the kingdom of God, for the healing of the sick, the liberation of the humiliated, and the forgiveness of sins was bound to come up against its most intransigent enemies – the priests of his people and the Roman occupying power. The journey to Jerusalem was heavy with foreboding: 'The Son of man must suffer many things, and be rejected' (Mark 8.31). So Christ leaves his friends free to decide whether they will go with him or not. 'If any man would come after me, let him deny himself and take up his cross and follow me.' Yet his entry into Jerusalem was after all a triumphal one. The people gathered together, crying, 'Blessed is he who comes in the name of the Lord! Blessed is the kingdom of our father David that is coming!' (Mark 11.9f.). This makes the nervousness of the forces of law and order all the more understandable, since they were afraid of a popular rising. The man from Nazareth was becoming dangerous, so he had better disappear swiftly and without more ado.

Up to now there is nothing out-of-the-way about this story. Many heroes, many freedom fighters, have faced death with open eyes for their people. They knew, or thought they knew, that their cause would be victorious none the less. For them, surrender to death was the most profound significance their life had to offer. They were ready to endure suffering for their passion, and to make the sacrifice required of them.

But in the case of Christ something different intervened, something which is initially quite incomprehensible. The night before the Romans arrested him, he went into the garden of Gethsemane, taking only three of his friends with him, and 'began to be greatly distressed and troubled,' as Mark writes. 'He began to be sorrowful and afraid,' Matthew reports. In fact 'he despaired'. 'My soul is very sorrowful, even to death,' he said, and begged his friends to stay awake with him.

Earlier, too, Christ had often withdrawn at night in order to be united in prayer with the God whom he always called so intimately 'my Father'. Here, for the first time, he does not want to be alone with God. He seeks protection among his friends. Protection from whom? And then comes the prayer that sounds like a demand: 'Father, all things are possible to thee; remove this cup from me' (Mark 14.36) – spare me this suffering. What suffering? In Matthew and Luke the prayer sounds somewhat more modest: 'If it be possible. . .' and 'If thou art willing', remove this cup from me.

Christ's request *was not granted*. God, his Father, rejected it. Elsewhere we are always told 'I and the Father are *one*.' But here Christ's communion with God seems to break down. That is why his friends fall into a deep sleep, as if they are paralysed by grief. In this severance Christ only holds on to his union with the God of his love and passion by transcending himself to say, 'Nevertheless'. '*Nevertheless* not my will but thine be done.' Christ's true passion begins with the prayer in Gethsemane which was not heard, which was rejected through the divine silence; for his true passion was his suffering from God. Of course there was also the simple human fear of pain. It would be cruel to claim that, as God's Son, Christ would have been unable to experience fear. But it would also be foolish to view him as a sensitive weakling who was overcome by lachrymose self-pity in the face of bodily torment and his swiftly approaching death.

I believe that it was a quite different fear which laid hold of Christ here and lacerated his soul. It was the fear that he, the only begotten Son, who loved the Father as no one had ever loved before, could be 'forsaken', 'rejected', even 'cursed' by that Father. He is not afraid for his life. He is afraid for God. He is afraid for the Father's kingdom, whose joy he had proclaimed to the poor.

This *suffering from God himself* is the real torment in Christ's passion. This godforsakenness is the cup which he is not spared. God's terrible silence in response to Christ's prayer in Gethsemane is more than a deathly stillness. It is echoed in the dark night of the soul, in which everything that makes life something living withers away, and in which hope vanishes. Martin Buber called it the eclipse of God.

Who can stay awake in this night of God? Who will not be as if paralysed by it? Jesus' friends were protected from its terrors by a profound sleep. Luke, the doctor, and other witnesses speak of a 'bloody sweat' which fell on the ground from the wakeful, imploring Christ. The Luther Bible heads this chapter 'The Struggle in Gethsemane'. The struggle with whom? Christ's struggle with himself? His struggle with death? I think it is more than that. It is Christ's struggle with God. This was his real agony. He overcame it through his self-surrender. That was his victory, and our hope.

We find the other story at the end of Christ's passion, on Golgotha, the place of execution. Again it is a prayer or, to be more exact, a despairing cry to God. 'And at the ninth hour Jesus cried with a loud voice, "Eloi, Eloi, lama sabachthani", which means, "My God, my God, why has thou forsaken me?" '

For three hours he hung nailed to the cross, apparently in silence, locked in agony and waiting for death. And then he died with this cry, which expresses the most profound abandonment by the God on whom he had pinned all his hopes and for whom he was hanging on the cross.

This must be the historical core of the Golgotha story. The idea that the last word the dying Son addressed to God his Father could possibly have been, 'You have forsaken me' – such an idea could never have taken root in the Christian faith had this terrible word not really been spoken, or had it not at least been perceptible from Jesus' death cry. We shall never be able to get used to the fact that at the very centre of the Christian faith we hear this cry of the godforsaken Christ for God. We shall always attempt to weaken its effect and to replace it by 'more pious' parting words – as was already done in the New Testament and the later history of the church. And yet: terrible though this death cry of Christ is, we feel obscurely that it is important for us – vitally important, even. For this is the cry in which so many tormented people can join, because it expresses their real situation: 'My God, why have you forsaken me?'

This saying does not become any easier to accept because it is taken from the opening of Psalm 22. The notion that the dying Jesus prayed the whole of the Psalm 22 on the cross is really unthinkable. For one thing, the psalm ends with a glorious prayer of thanksgiving for deliverance from death; and there was no deliverance on the cross. For another thing, after he had hung for a short time on the gibbet, the crucified Jesus was no longer capable of speech.

No, it is quite simply the cry of a person who has been forsaken, for the God who has left him in the lurch. Early manuscripts of Mark's Gospel put it even more drastically: 'Why have you exposed me to shame?' and, 'Why have you cursed me?' Even the much later Epistle to the Hebrews holds fast to this remembrance: 'Far from God – even without God – he tasted death for us all' (2.9). And it is only here on the cross that Christ no longer addresses God intimately as 'Father', but calls him 'God'; quite officially, as if he were forced to doubt whether he really was the Son of God the Father.

What Christ was afraid of, what he wrestled with in Gethsemane, what he implored the Father to save him from, was not spared him. It happened on the cross. The Father forsook the Son and 'God is silent'. The Son was forsaken by the Father, rejected and cursed. He bore the judgment in which everyone is alone and in which no one can stand.

Is there any answer to the question *why* God forsook him? Is there any answer to these agonizing questionings of disappointment and death: 'My God, Why? Why. . . ?'

Ever since the New Testament, Christian theology has evolved a whole series of answers, which wring permanent significance out of

Christ's death. He suffered vicariously for us. He died as an atoning sacrifice for our sins. All these answers of faith are certainly not wrong, but if we imagine them being offered as an answer to the dying Christ, crying out for God, then we sense immediately how inappropriate they are.

A real answer to the question, 'My God, why have you forsaken me?' cannot be a theoretical answer beginning with the word 'Because'. It has to be a practical answer. An experience of this kind can only be answered by another experience, not by an explanation. A reality like this can be answered only by another reality. And surely there is really only *one* satisfying and liberating answer to the question, 'My God, why have you forsaken me?' It is the answer of the resurrection: 'For a brief moment I forsook you, but with great compassion I will gather you.' Every other answer would fall short, either giving death eternal significance, or failing to take it seriously. The only answer to this death of the Son in godforsakenness is: 'Death is swallowed up in victory' (I Cor. 15.55). There is only this answer to the questions that torment us – only this answer, or none at all.

At the centre of the Christian faith is the history of Christ's passion. At the centre of this passion is the experience of God endured by the Godforsaken, God-cursed Christ. Is this the end of all human and religious hope? Or is it the beginning of the true hope, which has been born again and can no longer be shaken?

For me it is the beginning of true hope, because it is the beginning of a life which has death behind it and for which hell is no longer to be feared.

At the point where men and women lose hope, where they become powerless and can do nothing more, the lonely, assailed and forsaken Christ waits for them and gives them a share in his passion.

At the point where men and women betray their hope and chase after illusions, where they violate the future and their neighbours – there stands Christ, praying, crying out and wrestling for the will of God; and he gives them a share in his suffering.

Only the person who has himself suffered can help other sufferers; that is an ancient truth. Otherwise one would not even be able to understand the suffering person. So in our difficulties we always turn only to people who we think know the straits we are in, because they have gone through the same thing themselves.

The passionately loving Christ, the persecuted Christ, the lonely Christ, the Christ despairing over God's silence, the Christ who in dying was so totally forsaken, for us and for our sakes, is like the brother or the friend to whom one can confide *everything*, because he knows everything and has suffered everything that can happen to us – and more.

In our hopes about life, in our activity, in our love of living, we participate in his passion for the kingdom of freedom.

Our disappointments, our lonelinesses and our defeats do not separate us from him; they draw us more deeply into communion with him. And with the final unanswered cry, 'Why, my God, why?' we join in his death cry and await with him the resurrection.

This is what faith really is: believing, not with the head or the lips or out of habit, but believing *with one's whole life*. It means seeking community with the human Christ in every situation in life, and in every situation experiencing his own history. Good Friday is the most comprehensive and most profound expression of Christ's fellowship with every human being.

That is why it is true to say: *Ave crux, unica spes*. The Christ who for us and for our sakes was lonely, despairing and forsaken, is our true hope. In him the despair that oppresses us becomes free to hope. The arrogance with which we hinder ourselves and other people melts away, and we become as open and as vulnerable as he was.

What initially seemed so meaningless and so irreconcilable – our hope and Christ's cross – belong together as a single whole, just as do the passionate hope for life and the readiness for disappointment, pain and death.

Beneath the cross of Christ hope is born again out of the depths. The person who has once sensed this is never afraid of any depths again. His hope has become firm and unconquerable. Let me close with an acknowledgment of hope that comes from the civil war in Northern Ireland. It was written by a friend, Gordon Gray, a Protestant minister belonging to the movement for reconciliation:

Father, I am a man of my time.
Around me I see the signs and symbols of man's
     fear,
         hatred,
             alienation.
A bomb exploding in a crowded market square,
demagogic faces on TV twisted in mocking confrontation.

My hopes have been destroyed.
The death of things I hoped for
has been celebrated by others as victory in your power.
Father, can this be so?

I am perplexed, angry, hopeless, sick.
'Hope deferred maketh the heart sick.'
I want to turn my back,
     wash my hands,
         save my self, my family,
             get out.

But every time I turn to go,
there stands in my way
a Cross, calling me back.
Father, how much, at times, I have
resented that Cross
that stands between me and my personal future.
I am a prisoner.

The *empty* cross! Where is the one who hung there?
There!
     standing on the horizon, in the ruins,
     beckoning me to venture with him.
Lord, I am a prisoner – of hope!

15 Easter: The Festal Protest against Death

Death is swallowed up in victory.
O death, where is thy sting?
O grave, where is thy victory?
The sting of death is sin;
and the strength of sin is the law.
But thanks be to God, who giveth us the victory
through our Lord Jesus Christ (I Cor. 15.54–57).

With these unforgettable words Paul celebrates the victory of life over death and sin, which make a hell out of life in this world. But we do not find it so easy to bring ourselves to utter this song of liberty.

'I live among middle-class English people,' said one member of the Ecumenical Conference in Accra in 1974. 'They are well educated, have nice houses, a secure income and often a happy family life. They pin their hopes on the preservation of society as it was.' But in the present economic crisis their hope is being replaced by a deep-seated cynicism: 'Life is meaningless, and anyone who claims that it has a meaning is either a fool who shuts his eyes to reality, or a scoundrel who is exploiting human credulity for his own purposes.'

'Can one celebrate life in the midst of death?' our Argentinian friends asked us at Christmas 1978. 'For those of us who are living in this huge Latin American continent and try to pass on the witness to Christ there, this question is no empty phrase. We do not just encounter death here in the framework of subversive violence and repressive counter-measures which claim their victims every day. It creeps insidiously upon us much more cruelly in the form of increasing unemployment, the decline in the real wages of the poorest of the poor, and in the rise of infant mortality.' So we have to ask ourselves whether we can really celebrate the victory of the risen Christ, or whether we should not rather weep for the triumph of Pilate and all the tyrants who followed him in history.

In the prosperity of the industrial West today many people are becoming cynical. They close their eyes and do not want to see the misery of the 'Third World'. They stop their ears and do not want to hear the cry from the depths. They only want to keep what they have. And yet they sense how meaningless their lives are becoming.

In the terror of the 'Third World', people are being driven to despair. Every day they see violent death, and are pinned to the ground, helpless. They cry out and become apathetic because no one hears.

Both these experiences seem to contradict Christ's resurrection. Victory seems swallowed up in death, and hell triumphs – not only at the end of this life, but here and now, in many countries, through the mass use of torture.

Seen against the background of humanity's history of suffering, Easter is absurd and the resurrection of Jesus has no evidence to support it; for in this perspective of history, the power of death is unbroken. Even Paul saw more crosses in his lifetime, and went through more persecutions, than he had Easter experiences.

But things are quite different if, like Paul and the first Easter witnesses, we learn to see the everyday history of suffering in the perspective of Christ's resurrection. Then it begins to be absurd to see violence and death as a matter of course. Nothing is inevitable. Nothing has to be put up with. Then faith does not simply mean considering Christ's resurrection to be true and hoping for a life after death. Faith then means first of all getting up oneself and participating in God's creative power. God makes the impossible possible. He calls into existence the things that do not exist (Rom. 4.17). He is the Creator.

The Easter faith recognizes that the raising of the crucified Christ from the dead provides the great alternative to this world of death. This faith sees the raising of Christ as God's protest against death, and against all the people who work for death; for the Easter faith recognizes God's passion for the life of the person who is threatened by death and with death. And faith participates in this process of love by getting up out of the apathy of misery and out of the cynicism of prosperity, and fighting against death's accomplices, here and now, in this life.

Weary Christians have often enough deleted this critical and liberating power from Easter. Their faith has then degenerated into the confident belief in certain facts, and a poverty-stricken hope for the next world, as if death were nothing but a fate we meet with at the end of life. But death is an evil power now, in life's very midst. It is the economic death of the person we allow to starve; the political death of the people who are oppressed; the social death of the handicapped; the noisy death that strikes through napalm bombs and torture; and the soundless death of the apathetic soul.

The resurrection faith is not proved true by means of historical evidence, or only in the next world. It is proved here and now, through the courage for revolt, the protest against deadly powers, and the self-giving of men and women for the victory of life. It is impossible to talk convincingly about Christ's resurrection without participating in the movement of the Spirit 'who descends on all flesh' to quicken it. This movement of the Spirit is the divine 'liberation movement', for it is the process whereby the world is recreated.

So resurrection means rebirth out of impotence and indolence to 'the living hope'. And today 'living hope' means a passion for life, and a lived protest against death.

The person who does not contest with the lords of this world their right to that world does not arrive at the certainty that in the end death will be swallowed up in victory. The resurrection hope is a hope which only makes sense beneath the cross, that is, in the resistance of love against death. It is this that is behind the poem written by the Swiss pastor Kurt Marti:

That could just suit many a master. . .
But a resurrection is coming,
different, quite different, from any we imagined.
A resurrection is coming which is
God's rebellion against the masters,
and the master of the masters, death.

Christ's resurrection is the beginning of God's rebellion. That rebellion is still going on in the Spirit of hope, and will be completed when, together with death, 'every rule and every authority and power' is at last abolished (I Cor. 15.24).

The resurrection hope finds living expression in men and women when they *protest* against death and the slaves of death. But it lives from something different – from the superabundance of God's future. Its freedom lives in resistance against all the outward and inward denials of life. But it does not live from this protest. It lives from joy in the coming victory of life. 'How much more' the apostle often says, when he is talking, not about liberation *from* sin, law and death, but about freedom *for* life, for righteousness, for glory. We might call this 'the added value' of hope. It is 'the surplus' of Christ's resurrection in the powers of liberation. The 'nevertheless' with which we resist evil and our own resignation is only the sombre reverse side of the 'how much more' of the hope that quickens us. Protest and resistance are founded on this hope. Otherwise they degenerate into mere accusation and campaigns of revenge. But the greater hope has to take living form in this protest and resistance; otherwise it turns into religious seduction.

Where is this 'added value' of hope alive, and how do people experience it? Easter is a feast, and it is as the feast of freedom that it is celebrated. For with Easter begins the laughter of the redeemed, the dance of the liberated and the creative play of fantasy. From time immemorial Easter hymns have celebrated the victory of life by laughing at death, mocking at hell, and ridiculing the mighty ones who spread fear and terror round about them. Easter sermons used once to begin with good jokes. There is a rabbinic saying that 'Anyone who makes a person laugh, opens heaven to him.'

Easter is a liberating feast. Where it is celebrated, people must eat and drink. The resurrection cannot be celebrated without the eucharist. The *shalom* meal which follows confers fellowship – fellowship with the people who are hungry and thirsty. So everyone should be invited to share our bread, so as to find this new community. This is true on a world-wide scale as well. Easter celebrations in the industrial West are not real feasts, simply because we do not see to it that we bear an equal share of the burdens of the hungry nations. One can hardly celebrate a feast, with eating and drinking, behind locked doors, with armed guards in front of them.

Easter is the feast of freedom. It makes the life which it touches a *festal* life. 'The risen Christ makes life a perpetual feast,' said Athanasius. But can the whole of life really be a feast? Even life's dark side – death, guilt, senseless suffering? I think it can. Once we

realize that the giver of this feast is the outcast, suffering, crucified
Son of man from Nazareth, then every 'no' is absorbed into this
profound 'yes', and is swallowed up in its victory.

Easter is at one and the same time God's protest *against* death, and
the feast of freedom *from* death. Anyone who fails to hold these two
things together has failed to understand the resurrection of the Christ
who was crucified. Resistance is the protest of those who hope, and
hope is the feast of the people who resist.

Anyone who makes a person laugh
opens heaven to him.
Anyone who is patient with another
gives him a future.
Anyone who accepts a person
as he himself
is accepted by Christ
loosens his tongue for life's hymn of praise.

Let us go out
from our customs and our habits
and learn to hope from the Bible.
Let us go out
and cross the frontiers
so that we may infect life with hope.
Let us ignore the barriers,
and look only to the One who breaks them down.
He is risen.
Jesus is risen indeed.
Blessed be the Lord for ever and ever.

16 Pentecost: There is Enough for Everyone

And when they had prayed, the place in which they were gathered together was shaken; and they were all filled with the Holy Spirit and spoke the word of God with rejoicing.

Now the company of those who believed were of one heart and soul, and no one said that any of the things which he possessed was his own, but they had everything in common.

And with great power the apostles gave their testimony to the resurrrection of the Lord Jesus, and great grace was upon them all.

There was not a needy person among them, for as many as were possessors of lands or houses sold them, and brought the proceeds of what was sold and laid it at the apostles' feet; and distribution was made to each as any had need (Acts 4.31–35).

Prayer
Come God, Holy Spirit,
come to our threatened and plundered world.
Come to us, for we are frightened and fainthearted.
Spirit of life,
fill us with the livingness of your eternal life.
Spirit of eternal blessedness,
fill us with your joy in living.
Spirit of love,
fill our world with your righteousness.
Ever-present God, in your presence we too are wholly present.
Creative God, in your strength we too discover our energies.
God whose life is fellowship, you come among us,
and in you we find one another
and become one heart and soul.

Take from us our fear of death, free us from our greed for life.
Assert the rights of the poor, and convert the mighty.
Raise the oppressed
and make the lords of this world brothers,
so that we may find you in our community with one another
and praise you together, one with another:
God, Holy Spirit, proceeding from the Father, whose light
shines forth in the Son, and who draws the whole world into
the fellowship of the triune God.

There is enough for everyone: that is the incredible message of this
first Pentecost story. We are not being told some story about 'the
golden age' of the first Christians long ago. This is the announcement
to us today about real, possible ways of living in the superfluity of the
creative Spirit. It is a message through which we ourselves can arrive
at a new experience: the experience of the community of the Spirit.

There is enough for everyone: but ten per cent of the people in this
country are living beneath subsistence level. That is the poverty
existing in the affluent society of West Germany. How do these things
fit together?

There is enough for everyone: but 450 million people in the world
are hungry, and 77 nations are on the wealthy countries' lists for
development aid. How does that make sense?

There is enough for everyone: but millions of men and women are
unable to find work. Mineral resources are getting scarcer and
scarcer. Sources of energy are drying up. Prices are rising. Debts are
increasing. Want is spreading in all areas of life. What a contradiction!

How can there be 'enough for everyone', when we know that from
the very beginning men and women have lived with want, with empty
stomachs and thirsty throats, with anxiety in their hearts and fear at
their backs? If men and women have always had to live like this in the
past, and will certainly have to go on living like this in the future?
There has never been enough, there still is not enough, and there
never will be enough: surely that has to be our indignant answer? But
are we right? Were the first Christians really just talking nonsense?
What is the truth?

The Pentecost story is talking about an experience of God. It is the experience of the Spirit who descends on men and women, permeates them through and through, soul and body, and brings them to a new community and fellowship with one another. In this experience people discover that they are filled with new energies they had never imagined to exist, and find the courage for a new style of living. That is why this Spirit is called the creative Spirit, the life-giving Spirit, the Spirit of the resurrection – in fact *the Holy Spirit*.

It is a remarkable thing, but whenever people in the New Testament talk about this experience of God in the creative Spirit, they become intoxicated and fall into superlatives. They talk about 'the abundance' of the Spirit, 'the overflowing exhuberance' of the Spirit, about the boundless 'riches of life'. 'In every way you are enriched, so that you are not lacking in any gift', Paul told the little group of Christians among the dock-workers in Corinth (I Cor. 1.5,7). People later called the Christian community in Jerusalem 'the poor'; but in our text we are told that 'there was not a needy person among them' (Acts 4.34). Everybody has enough, more than enough, and there is no want any more, not in any way. This is the unanimous experience of life in the Spirit, in the creative, life-giving, Holy Spirit.

How does it happen? Is it realistic, or just a kind of religious ecstasy? Is it a possibility we can actually experience? Something we can really put into practice? Or is it nothing more than the expression of a religious longing?

We find three factors in our story for the fullness of life and the overcoming of every want:

1. 'And with great power the apostles gave their testimony to the resurrection of the Lord Jesus, and great grace was upon them all.' That is the first thing, for that is the beginning of everything else. It is the resurrection of the crucified Christ from the dead that opens up the fullness of life – of eternally living life. Death's power has been taken away. The menaces of death have already ceased to be effective. Immortal life and life's indestructible joys are already present, here and now. Everyone can enjoy 'eternal life and blessedness'. Everyone can have them both, for nothing – simply through grace. The risen Christ gives the divine life to everybody who enters into the community of his people and believes.

To be in want means to be shut out from the pleasures of life. To be in want means not to have enough to eat and drink. To be in want means to be sick and lonely. In the ultimate resort, to suffer want means to lose life itself. The greatest want of all, the absolute deprivation, is death. All the other wants we experience and suffer from in life are connected with death. They are all something death steals from life. Because we know we have to die, we cannot get enough of living.

But if Christ is risen, then this means the spread of hope for the life that is immortal, a life no death can kill, a life of which there is always enough, more than enough, not just for those of us who are still alive, but for the dead as well. Both in our lives and in our deaths we partake of this indestructible resurrection life which has become manifest through Christ. 'If we live, we live to the Lord, and if we die, we die to the Lord; so then, whether we live or whether we die, we are the Lord's' (Rom. 14.8).

Pentecost has Easter as its premise. The experience of the creative and therefore immortal spirit of life in us is nothing other than the new experience of the whole of life in the light of the resurrection. For this experience of the Spirit is the feast of a life that conquers death. It is the feast of a life that no longer knows any want. It is the feast of the rapturous, overflowing divine joy of living.

2. 'Now the company of those who believed were of one heart and soul.' That is the second factor, and it takes us a step further. Men and women, quite unknown to one another, become believers, and these people are at once 'of one heart and soul'. This is what the experience of the Spirit of fellowship means. The Spirit of fellowship is the God among us. In him the divisions between people and our enmity towards one another are overcome. The oppression of people by other people stops. The humiliation of people by other people comes to an end. The estrangement of one person from another is swept away. Masters and servants become brothers. Men and women become friends. Privileges and discriminations disappear from human society. We become 'of one heart and soul'.

Wherever this happens we experience God: the God among us, the God who is community and fellowship, the Holy Spirit.

How is this possible? The secret is very simple. Whenever God, the fountain and source of life and all goodly powers, ceases to be a God far away in heaven and becomes present among us, then there is no longer any want. But where there is no longer any want, there is no longer any struggle for power either, and no more rivalry. And where there is no struggle for power and no rivalry, the age-old fears of one another we have built up simply fall away, and so do our desperately bottled-up aggressions. We step out into free life. Our fears and our aggressions simply become ludicrous, because there is enough for everyone there. God himself is there. He lives among us and invites us through his Spirit of fellowship to become 'of one heart and soul'.

3. 'No one said that any of the things which he possessed was his own, but they had everything in common.' This is the third point, and everything else comes down to this. In the resurrection hope and in the experience of the God of community and fellowship, no one needs to cling to his possessions any longer. Anyone who has found the assurance of eternal life no longer needs the ambiguous security that his possessions give him. So all his possessions are there to be used by the people who need them. That is why 'they had everything in common' and that is why there was not 'a needy person among them'. They brought everything they had to the apostles and gave 'to each as any had need'.

This first Pentecost congregation had enough to satisfy life's elemental needs – more than enough. The community of Christ always has enough to satisfy life's elemental needs – more than enough. The emperor Julian the Apostate said about the community of Christians in Rome three hundred years later: 'These Christians do not merely feed their own poor; they feed the poor of the whole city as well.' None of these people were rich, and yet they lived in superfluity.

Why does the Pentecost community always have 'more than enough'? Because the power of the resurrection and the Spirit of fellowship have liberated them from the fear of death and from anxiety about life. If God is for us, if God is in our midst, between each and all of us, then there is no longer any want, in any sector of life. People share everything and share *in* everything, *di*vide and *con*fide all that they have. That is the message of the Pentecost community in Jerusalem, which made so many rich. And that is their message to us as well.

Some smart people are critical about this story. They say: 'Oh well, yes, of course – that was primitive Christian communism. But it didn't work out in the long run. Human beings just are wicked by nature. They need property because they're egoists. So let's stick to healthy egoism!' They do not realize how banal – how literally lacking in spirit – their criticism is.

It is of course true that, when we look at our world, we can see that exactly the opposite principle dominates our lives, our thinking, our economy and our politics. In all these sectors of life the slogan is 'never enough!' Our economy is based on wants. We assume that there are wants everywhere, wants which can only be met by work and still more work, by stepping up production, and by more and more mass products. For everyone who has to run an economy knows that he has to meet increasing demands with a scarcity of goods. And he knows too that the race between growing demand and never-quite-adequate supply is a race he can never win.

There is never enough for everybody: that is why we have the struggle for oil, the struggle for raw materials, the struggle for world markets, the struggle for educational opportunities and jobs, the permanent hunt after money and pleasure.

Of course there are natural, basic wants which have to be satisfied if people are to live and to live in decent and humane conditions. But our economy has left these basic needs far behind. It is not these natural requirements that dominate our lives and provide the driving power for our economy; it is demands that have been artificially stimulated and heightened. These additional desires are in principle limitless. They can be stepped up beyond any possible fulfilment. Why? In our modern society human beings have apparently been turned into voracious monsters. They are tormented by an unquenchable thirst for life. They are possessed by an insatiable hunger for power. The more they have, the more they want, so their appetite is endless and can never be appeased.

Why have people in our modern world become so distorted? Because both consciously and unconsciously they are dominated by the fear of death. For a person's greed for life is really his fear of death; and his fear of death finds expression in an unbridled hunger for power. 'You only live once!' we are told. You might miss out on something! This hunger for pleasure, for possessions, for power – this thirst for recognition by way of success and admiration – this is the sin of modern men and women. This is their godlessness and their godforsakenness. The person who loses God makes a god out of himself. 'The one who lost what you lost, stops at nothing,' said Nietzsche. And so human beings have turned into proud and unhappy mini-gods.

There is never enough for everyone. So reach out now and help yourself! This is what death tells us – death which will swallow us up after we have swallowed up everything else. Our modern economy based on want, our modern ideology of growth and the compulsion to expand are pacts with death. They are deadly games with human anxiety. They are bets placed on the craving for life, and they are sucking people dry.

There is not enough for everybody. That is why we have competition and rivalry – in our schools for the best marks, in our universities for the courses that promise the most lucrative careers, in our working lives for secure jobs and rising incomes. We even compete with one another for the most attractive places in which to spend our holidays.

There is not enough for everyone: this motto shatters every human community and rouses one nation against another, one class against another, one sex against the other; and in the end everybody against everybody else, and everyone against his own self. It is a slogan of fear which makes people lonely and leads them into a world which is in principle hostile. 'Every man for himself!' people say. If you don't push, if you go to the back of the queue, that's your own fault. Everyone is his own best friend. And so we have a world that really is without heart and without soul.

Finally, this deadly craving for life and this struggle of each against everyone is the very state of affairs we find ourselves in today, when ten per cent of our own people are living in poverty, 450 million people in the world are hungry, and the nations of the Third World are falling deeper and deeper into debt. This is really no wonder. And it is not a natural disaster either. These poor nations are 'underdeveloped' because they have been 'de-developed' – dragged down by the wealthy nations of the world. They are hungry because they are being starved. They are getting poorer because they are being forced into debt. They are not suffering because of some deficiency of nature. They are suffering from the injustice of other people, the unequal distribution of goods, and the inequality of opportunity in life. One can live in poverty, one can live with poverty. When poverty is shared, it is bearable. It is only injustice that turns want into a torment, and being deprived of one's rights that makes poverty into a hell.

If we want to find true life, and to escape the universal death of the world – if we want to gain the true riches of life and escape from poverty and want, then we must turn round and begin at the point where the severest loss of all begins: with God. Godlessness leads to the feeling of godforsakenness. Godforsakenness lets the fear of death and the devouring lust for life well up in us; and then there is never enough. But if God is not far off; if he is near; if he is present among us in the Spirit, then we find a new, indescribable joy in living. We are in safekeeping; we are at home; we are trusted and can trust ourselves and other people. Our profoundest want, the want of God, has been remedied. Our yearning for happiness has been fulfilled. We are blissful and content.

God is present in his Spirit. We have to understand this as meaning that God is present in our lives as the *living* God. Our limited, vulnerable and mortal lives are encompassed and penetrated through and through by his life, which is unlimited, glorious and eternal. With all the perceptions of our minds and spirits, with all the impulses of our souls, and all the needs and urges of our bodies, we participate in, we are drawn into, the eternal divine life. In our existence we sense God's existence; in our suffering we feel his pain; in our happiness we meet the assent of his bliss. God is present in his Spirit. 'In him we live and move and have our being.' Everyone who experiences and realizes this, discovers how calm and relaxed he becomes, because he ceases to be afraid.

When the fear of death leaves us, the destructive craving for life leaves us too. We can then restrict our desires and our demands to our natural requirements. The dreams of power and happiness and luxury and far-off places, which are used to create artificial wants, no longer entice us. They have become ludicrous. So we shall use only what we really need, and shall no longer be prepared to go along with the lunacy of extravagance and waste. For this we do not even need solemn appeals for saving and moderation; for life itself is glorious, and here joy in existence can be had for nothing.

This means that the best thing we can do is to build up communities, and to strengthen our sense of the common life we share with one another and for one another. The ideology of 'there is never enough for everyone' makes people lonely. It isolates them and robs them of relationships. But in community we become rich – rich in friends, in neighbours, in colleagues, in comrades, in brothers and sisters. Together, as a community, we can help ourselves in most of our difficulties. For after all, there are enough people and enough ideas, capabilities and energies to be had. They are only lying fallow, or are stunted and suppressed. So let us discover our wealth; let us discover our solidarity; let us build up communities. Let us take our lives into our own hands, and at long last out of the hands of the people who want to dominate and exploit us.

All really helpful projects or campaigns grew up out of spontaneous grass-roots communities, not from above: neighbourly help, help for the poor and sick, and so forth. The community of Christians can become the source of imaginative social service and continually new initiatives for life and living. It has not always been this source, unfortunately; but it *can* be – provided that it is a Pentecost community. In the great bureaucratic organizations of society, the state and the churches, there is always want. But in the voluntary coming together of men and women at the grass-roots level, life's true wealth is experienced. Once all the nations have been given the liberty to provide for themselves, before they produce for the major world powers, then there will be enough for everyone to be satisfied.

There is enough for everybody when the justice of God is added to the fullness of life, to the abundance of life's powers, and to the adequacy of the means of living. It is this divine justice that ensures that everyone receives 'as each has any need' – no less, and no more. The fact that economic growth is up against its 'limits' is not the problem. The problem is the growth itself, and the fact that it is not really in our common interests. The divine righteousness and justice in spirit and life satisfies everyone. Then there is no more talk about 'growth', because there is no longer any want.

But the fullness of the divine life makes us hungry, insatiably hungry, in a different way. And in a different way it makes us thirsty, unquenchably thirsty: 'Blessed are those who hunger and thirst for righteousness.' This is the sector where our tasks for the future are to be found: in the growth and spread of social righteousness and justice in our nations, and among the poor and the rich peoples in the world. The poor are crying out for justice, not for prosperity; and we ourselves are perishing from injustice, even if we are leading pleasant, comfortable lives. The hunger for justice is a holy hunger; the thirst for justice is a sacred thirst. It is the hunger and thirst of the Holy Spirit himself. May that spirit fill us through and through.

17 The Liberation and Acceptance of the Handicapped

When I was asked a year ago by the Diakonisches Werk* whether I was willing to give this lecture at the combined conference of the handicapped and non-handicapped, my spontaneous response was to say 'yes'. Yes, a meeting of this kind is necessary in our society, which thoughtlessly and unfeelingly forces so many people on to the fringes of life, and handicaps them. I have been personally engaged in questions about the rehabilitation of the handicapped for a number of years. I have talked to many people who despair, and yet try to overcome that despair. I feel that this is my personal concern.

Then, at the beginning of this year, I wrote and tried to withdraw. No, I wrote, the matter itself is necessary, but I am not the proper person for it: I myself am not handicapped. It should not always be the non-handicapped who talk about the problems of the handicapped. Let the people who are handicapped do the talking themselves! Take them seriously in their human dignity! So I suggested that a handicapped person should speak for the handicapped themselves here.

Having said yes, because the matter itself is so important, and then no, because of my own limitations, I finally said, 'Very well: I will come after all. But I do not want to talk as a non-handicapped person to people who are handicapped. I should like to try to talk as a person to other people, and as a Christian to my sisters and brothers.'

I have come here with the conviction that there is really no such thing as 'the handicapped'. There are only people – people who have this or that difficulty, which makes the society of the strong and capable unjustly label them as 'handicapped', and exclude them more or less from public life. But these are people with the same human

* German Protestant organization for charitable work.

dignity and the same human rights as everyone else. So let us stop concentrating on another person's difficulties, and nailing him down to his problems by calling him a 'handicapped' person. Let us begin to discover the other *person* in the man or woman who is 'handicapped'. And let us respect that person's dignity, for he is just like you and me. It is in order to express this that I have come here; and I would beg you to accept me as I am, and to listen to me in what I can say, and to forgive me for what I am not able to say; and in this way to respect my limitations, too.

The over-riding theme chosen for this conference is the central and vitally important Christian commandment: accept one another. I have not a word of criticism. But I believe that *liberation of oneself* comes before mutual acceptance. We can only accept other people if we have first found ourselves. We can only accept other people if we have first freed ourselves from everything that oppresses and estranges us, and from everything that makes us small and ugly and worthless in our own eyes. Accept one another: this presupposes that we have found our independence, our dignity and our self-confidence, and are therefore acting freely and can confer freedom on each other through our mutual acceptance. Only the person who has found himself can accept other people, without being oppressive and a burden to them. Only the person who respects himself can allow himself to be helped by someone else without feeling humiliated and mortified. Anyone who has a firm confidence in himself does not need to be ashamed of anything, ever. I should like to talk a little about this freedom of mind and spirit before I go on to discuss the commandment that springs out of this freedom – acceptance of the other person.

Love your neighbour as yourself: that is the commandment of humanity given us by the Bible. We are used to looking only at the first part of the sentence: love your neighbour. But the second part belongs to it too. In fact it is actually the presupposition for the first part: love your neighbour *as yourself*. So I should love myself; and it is in the same way that I love myself that I should love my neighbour.

Self-love is not forbidden or condemned by the commandment of love. It is permitted, encouraged and presupposed as a matter of course. Self-love is the standard by which to measure love of our neighbour, and the power which inspires it. Self-love is the first thing, and love of our neighbour the second. Self-love is the secret of happiness and liberty, in our own lives and in our dealings with one another.

How can anyone who does not love himself love his neighbour? How can anyone who cannot endure himself endure his neighbour? Will not someone who loathes himself despise other people too? Will not someone who is filled with rage against himself and his destiny also want to destroy everything round him in his aggression? Will not the person who hates himself hate his neighbour too?

Self-hate is one of the torments of hell, for self-hate is the force of destruction. Self-love, on the other hand, is the power of heaven which makes everyone free and happy. Self-love in the true sense has nothing whatsoever to do with selfishness. Selfishness has its genesis in the fear of not getting one's fair share. It is a struggle through which people make life hell for themselves and others, and destroy all the delights life has to offer. Selfishness is not self-love at all but merely another variety of self-hate. Depression and aggression are closely related to one another. And in the same way self-seeking and self-hate are only two different sides of the same thing: self-love that has got lost. It is at this point that a person can begin to be free for open humanity towards other people: love yourself, for you are good. Respect yourself, for you have your own dignity. Be your own friend. So I shall begin with self-love, and only go on to love of our neighbour later.

Before we talk about the integration of the handicapped into society, and the life we share together, let us set out on the search for our own hidden value.

The liberation of people who are handicapped

Oppressed slaves have rebelled, fought against their masters and freed themselves. Exploited workers have given organized form to their solidarity in trade unions and have asserted their rights. Do people who are handicapped have to be liberated too?

There is such a thing as the liberation of the handicapped, and there has to be this liberation if people are to live with one another in a truly human sense. But here we have to make a distinction first of all. There are burdens which are imposed on people by others, and there are burdens which nature itself imposes. There are congenital and life-long disabilities which cannot be corrected or removed. That is true. One has to learn to live with them and to love oneself in them.

But there is also the unjust disabling of people already handicapped by nature. These unjust handicaps are those imposed by other people, and by the laws determining public life in this society of non-handicapped people. None of us must rest content with this handi-capping of the already handicapped. It is an injustice which cannot be endured, either by the handicapped or the non-handicapped. Pastor Ulrich Bach rightly distinguishes between 'being at a disad-vantage' because of a handicap and 'being put at a disadvantage' by a society determined by other people. We have to free ourselves from this handicapping of the handicapped in society – scandalous because it is unnecessary – and we all have to do it together, handicapped and non-handicapped alike, so that this divided society may become a more humane community.

At the same time, the social liberation of the handicapped is not to be achieved pre-eminently through the good will of people who are not handicapped. It will come about through the efforts of the handicapped themselves. It is only then, and only after that, that non-handicapped people who are free enough, and capable of listening to what the handicapped say, can make their contribution. It is not merely *permissible* for handicapped people to protest against their social discrimination and to fight against the mental humiliation they suffer because of the prejudices of other people. They *must* protest and fight. Anyone who does not protest here gives himself up for lost. The protest of the handicapped against their social handi-capping is an expression of love – self-love and neighbourly love.

It is a sign of hope that this year the voices of handicapped people in this country were raised – strident and harsh in tone, but at long last not to be ignored. 'Adapt yourselves, because you are dependent on other people and can't get along without them.' This message has been preached to the handicapped for too long. They have had to learn to play the part of the meek and eternally grateful, in order to survive in the world of the capable. They have often been treated as if they were children who have not yet come of age. All that was left to them was grief over their fate and silent self-pity. But this only teaches one to despise oneself. It does not teach self-confidence.

Everyone – and this is true of the handicapped person too – is probably capable of more than he thinks. Why? Because we believe we are incapable of so many things only because we are afraid of being defeated. But anyone who crawls into his own shell out of fear, never learns to try out his own potentialities, and to stretch them to the full. We only learn where our limitations really begin when we try to go beyond them.

There are people who always think that everything is impossible. 'It's useless,' they say from the start. 'It won't be any good,' and, 'I can't.' In this way they save themselves conflict, and a lot of pain, and some defeats. But they never experience anything of real life either. On the other hand, there are people who believe in the possible. 'All things are possible with God'; this is the tremendous confidence with which they pray. And 'all things are possible to him who believes'. In the power of this conviction they learn what their potentialities for living really are. Of course they experience disappointments and defeats. But they have the strength of soul which enables them to get up again after every setback. Anyone who starts to believe becomes a person with possibilities. Then he no longer fits into any of the blueprints which are laid down for him. The handicapped are going to free themselves from the cut-and-dried role they are supposed to play in our society. This is quite possible, because the power of inhumane prejudices is the sham power of the paper tiger. The spectre quickly disappears once a few handicapped people cease to believe in it and break away.

It must unfortunately be said that it is at this point that the non-handicapped are most afraid of the handicapped. They are quite prepared to do everything *for* the handicapped, and to see that they lack for nothing. But they do not want to concede them independence, because they are afraid that they could harm themselves and other people. 'Freedom' and 'self-determination' and 'personal responsibility' have become foreign words for some handicapped people, because they are foreign to their families and the people who look after them.

How are the handicapped to become adult people? There is surely nothing in the world which incapacitates and humiliates a grown-up person more than to be continually kept in leading strings by his parents through incessant guidance and care. Of course the handicapped person needs the help of other people, and he can possess the inner freedom which will allow him to endure it. But even when sympathy is well meant, it can be insulting. It is insulting if it springs from the fear of letting the suffering of someone else come too close. There is a charitable love which helps the other person to exercise his own dignity and lead his own life. But there is also a disabling charity which prevents the very thing it should liberate and heal.

Part of charitable love is the wisdom to distinguish between responsibility for the needy person and respect for his or her personal life. Love, responsibility, care and help find their limits at the point where they infringe upon the independence of the other person. The responsibility we undertake for someone else must be withdrawn the moment the other person arrives at his own self, so that his own life begins to stir. Otherwise responsibility easily becomes a concealed form of domination.

Even Jesus did not come to bind other people to himself through his ministry to them, or to make himself indispensable. 'Your *faith* has helped you', he always said, when people wanted to thank him for their healing: you *own* faith. But if guidance is withdrawn because people have 'come of age', if responsibility is resigned, because the other person has quickened into life, what is left? Then solicitude ends and friendship begins. Then there are no longer helpers, there are no longer people in need of help. Then the handicapped and the non-handicapped are happy to live together, because each is vitally interested in the personal world of the other.

The final and most important point of all, however, is the liberation of handicapped people from despondency and sadness. Where does this inward burden come from? It comes from the prejudices of the capable and strong, which convey to the handicapped the paralysing feeling that they are judged as being of inferior value. It makes them, even in their own eyes, ugly, incapable and useless. But how can one be self-confident and free if one seems despicable to oneself?

Everything depends on discovering one's own life and *learning to love it*. This life is *my* life, this world is *my* world, this problem is *my* problem and this limitation is *my* limitation. Learning to love oneself, together with one's handicaps, in an environment where one meets with contempt and pity, requires tremendous independence and a totally new orientation.

In actual fact the distinction between the healthy and the handicapped does not exist. For every human life is limited, vulnerable and weak. Helpless we are born and helpless we die. So in reality there is no such thing as a non-handicapped life. It is only the ideal of health set up by the society of the capable which condemns a certain group of people to be called 'handicapped'.

In our society health means the capacity for work and the capacity
for enjoyment. Nothing else? No, practically nothing else. So anyone
who is incapable of working and limited in his capacity for enjoyment
counts as sick. To my mind this 'health' ideal is profoundly inhumane,
and humiliating for us all.

True health is something quite different. True health is the strength
to live, the strength to suffer, and the strength to die. Health is not a
condition of my body; it is the power of my soul to cope with the
varying condition of that body. How can we gain this power of soul,
and in what way can we strengthen it?

We gain and fortify this power of soul when we begin to love
ourselves. Self-love evokes strength of soul, and strength of soul gives
us the power to move mountains – or if we cannot move them, at
least to avoid capitulating in the face of them. But how does a person,
in his difficulties, come to love, and not to despise, himself?

Let me add a personal word here. In the misery of a dirty hut in a
prisoner-of-war camp in 1945 I lost all the hopes that had filled my
life up till then. I was overcome by a deadly depression. I became ill.
I didn't get up any more. I didn't want to go on living. But then a
miracle happened. Through the help of friends I won through to the
certainty: there is someone who loves you and believes in you. There
is someone who is waiting for you, someone to whom you are
infinitely important. Get up and go to meet him! The moment I began
to sense that there was someone who loved me and who did not give
me up, I crept out of my forlorn corner and began to love myself
again. My life – even life behind barbed wire – became important to
me once more, and I survived. I overcame my deadly sadness. What
had I learned in that situation? I had come to understand that because
God loves us, we should love ourselves. But even that is too general:
God loves every one of us just as he is – not as someone different –
simply as he is now. And so we can love what God loves – ourselves.
The person who goes on despising himself after that is really despising
God, not himself at all.

I know: to make the eternal God the lodestone for one's own tiny
feeling about life sounds easy. And I know, too, how difficult it is in
practice. But it is the only alternative to taking our bearings from a
society which rewards the capable and pushes the handicapped out.

The liberation of the non-handicapped

Disability always has two sides to it. On the one hand there is the person who is handicapped, and on the other the person who himself imposes a handicap. The handicapped person is robbed of his rights. That is inhumane. But the handicapper also robs himself of his own humanity, because he acts in an inhumane way. So in our society the non-handicapped person has to be liberated too. What does he have to be liberated from?

Here I shall only touch on one point, but it is an essential one. If they want to be truly human, people who are not themselves handicapped must be liberated from their illusion that they are healthy; and they must at the same time be freed from their fear of people who are handicapped. There have been many investigations into the attitude of the population to the physically and mentally handicapped. These studies continually point to insecurity and fear:

Ninety per cent do not know how they should behave towards handicapped people.

Fifty-six per cent would not like to live in the same house as a handicapped person.

Sixty-five per cent think that handicapped people ought to be housed in institutions.

Seventy per cent say that they feel uneasy and frightened when they see a handicapped person.

Seventy-two per cent are in favour of an abortion if a child shows signs of deformity; and so on.

In these studies, people's initial reaction is described as follows:

The equilibrium of the non-handicapped person is disturbed. The abnormal appearance of a deformed body does not fit into the stereotype people have of a human counterpart. The disharmonious outward appearance, which offends our aesthetic feelings, can lead to reactions of repulsion. . . The non-handicapped person is made to feel profoundly insecure. . . He does not succeed in discovering in his counterpart the human person first of all. He sees only the handicap, and generalizes this to cover the whole personality (Schmidt-Janzen, 1968).

It should be added in all fairness that this 'initial reaction' really is only the *first* reaction of many people, and that fear and insecurity can speedily be overcome when practicable ways are found of meeting handicapped people. Fear of the encounter disappears in the encounter itself, and only then (J. Seim). So more and more meetings must be sought and arranged.

None the less, this fear of the insecurity evoked by handicapped people calls up many defence mechanisms. Some of the handicapped are treated like lepers. In public life they are pushed out of sight, and where they appear, people run away. If they are seen in hotels or holiday resorts, others take their departure. When human recognition is replaced by practical care in institutions, where the handicapped are 'together with people like themselves', a defence mechanism of this kind can also be at work. Some people then compensate for their feelings of guilt by unduly generous donations to homes for the handicapped, in cash or kind. A fine line often divides wanting to be free from buying oneself free.

But the more the handicapped are kept out of the public eye, the less other people know about them. And the less that is known about their personal life, the greater the fear of them. It is this fear which prevents men and women from meeting handicapped people, and from sharing a common life with them.

If this fear is to be overcome, nothing less is required than a totally new attitude to life in general. As long as anxiety makes us strive after the ideals of health, virility, accomplishment and beauty, we will always develop defensive attitudes towards people who are weak, sick, ugly and handicapped. Anyone who equates being a person with being healthy does not want to see people who are sick. Anyone who identifies being a person with the strength for performance and accomplishment will despise people who are weak. Anyone who thinks that being beautiful is the same as being a person will view every handicap as ugly. But are these values – health, accomplishment and beauty – really human values? No, they actually make human beings inhuman, for they force us to suppress and deny our weaknesses.

This inhuman notion of what being human means is disconcerted by the encounter with people who are handicapped, and quite rightly so. Pride in their health, and the mania for performance cherished by people who think that they are capable and efficient, means that men and women who are weaker are repressed and viewed with contemptuous patronage. But how can a person base his confidence in his own value on his health, or the proper functioning of his body, without being overcome by the fear of losing these things? How can anyone consider himself to be just, good and up to the mark in every way, merely because he is not at the moment handicapped – when he knows at the bottom of his heart that this state of affairs cannot continue?

The insecurity which, for so many people, is communicated by the handicapped is a necessary and salutory insecurity. It shows how often idolatry and superstition prompts people's attitude to living. The insecurity we have been talking about can free us of this delusion. The handicapped make the inhumanity of the allegedly non-handicapped evident. They help us to achieve true humanity. For they compel us to stop basing our self-confidence on health and capability, and to seek it through trust in God. It is precisely the people who are 'healthy' but insecure who have to discover true self-confidence, so that they can become free from their self-seeking and their terrified self-hate. Here the handicapped can help like no one else. Again, this sounds easy, but is all the same difficult to live up to in actual practice. But it is the only alternative, in a society which has built its house on the sand of pride in health and the delusion of accomplishment – which is to say on the abyss of fear.

The human being – the image of the living God

What is a human being? Who is a human being, in the fullest sense of the word. Is this person or that still human? Many people ask questions like this. They ask them because they have a particular picture, an ideal of what a human being is like; and they judge according to their wishful thinking. But who ultimately lives up to his own dream of what he would like to be?

If we search for a Christian answer to this question, we must open the Gospels and read what they say. The first thing that strikes us then is the fact that in the Gospels people are presented as sick, poor and in need of help. We only have to set the Gospel picture over against the Greek ideal of a human being, bursting with health, strength and goodness, in order to sense the difference. In the Gospels sickness is part of the definition of the true person. For wherever the Saviour appears, the sick appear too. Jesus is surrounded by all the sicknesses and sorrows of humanity: the possessed, the blind, the deaf, the lame, people sick in body and mind, and sinners of every kind. Out of the dark corners of the cities and villages to which they had been banished, out of the wildernesses where they had been cast out, they appear and reveal themselves and what they are to Jesus. This is the way Jesus sees people, in their inward and their outward handicaps. Jesus does not comprehend us on our sunny side, where we are strong and capable, but on the shadow side where our weaknesses are to be found.

Why does Jesus see us like this? Why do the sick come to him? Because he manifests a life of infectious healing power. That is why we are told again and again, 'and he healed their sick', 'and he cast out demons'. Even sick people who only came near him, or merely touched the hem of his garment, were healed. But in what way does Jesus actually help the sick person? Through some magical power? It sometimes looks like that; but Jesus himself repeatedly says, 'Your faith has saved you.' 'Go, be it done for you as you have believed,' he says to the centurion of Capernaum, and his servant was healed at that very moment. These are not magical healings; they are *healings brought about by faith*. That is why we have to notice too that Jesus did not heal all the sick among his people, but only a few whom he met; but that these healings were intended as a sign of hope for many.

Let us ask again: through what does Jesus heal these sick people? In what does the healing power of his life consist? The answer is quite unexpected. We find it in Matthew 8.17:

> That evening they brought to him many who were possessed by demons; and he cast out the spirits with a word, and healed all who were sick. This was to fulfil what was spoken by the prophet Isaiah, 'He took our infirmities and bore our diseases'.

So Jesus' power to heal is found in his power to suffer. He does not heal by eliminating disease and abolishing it, but by taking our sicknesses upon himself. People are not healed through Jesus' supernatural powers; they are healed – through his wounds. This points us to the path of suffering he chose, and to the cross on Golgotha. Jesus' whole life was really a single progress along the stations of the cross that led from Bethlehem to Golgotha; and along this path of suffering and death for the salvation of the world, Jesus healed the sick, received lepers and cast out evil spirits. These are the 'signs and wonders' which accompany him on his way. *Golgotha* is the secret of Jesus' healing power. Many people discovered that before his death, and many have discovered it since. But no one discerned the secret manifested in Jesus' life and death more clearly than the prophet Isaiah, whom Matthew cites. In chapter 53, talking about the new Servant of God, he says:

> He had no form or comeliness
> that we should look at him,
> and no beauty
> that we should desire him.
> He was despised and rejected by men;
> a man of sorrows, and acquainted with grief;
> as one from whom men hide their faces
> he was despised;
> and we esteemed him not.
> Surely, he has borne our sickness
> and carried our sorrows
> . . . through his wounds we are healed.

Through his wounds we are healed. That is the real point. Jesus heals, not through his divinity but through his humanity; not through his superior power, but because he surrenders himself to our pains and our death. But how can his sufferings heal the suffering of others? How can people who are themselves wounded to death find healing in *his* wounds? If we think in terms of human skill it sounds nonsensical. But it sounds true and liberating if we look at God.

'What is not assumed is not healed.' This was a theological principle held in the patristic church. It was a principle for the understanding of the true humanity of the Son of God. In Jesus Christ, God himself became man. He took human nature on himself entirely and truly, and made it part of his own divine life. It was not merely the finite and mortal aspect of humanity that the eternal God accepted and made part of his life; it was also handicapped, sick, weak and helpless humanity, and people unfitted for living. He takes our handicaps on himself and makes them part of his own eternal life. He accepts our tears and makes them the expression of his own pain. This is how God heals all sicknesses and all griefs: by making every sickness and every grief his own suffering and his own grieving.

God accepts our life as it really is, and absorbs it into himself – only not the life we dream of, not our phantom life and our inhuman ideals. God accepts the whole of human nature in its infirmities, and heals it by communicating to it his eternal divine nature.

So healing consists of community, and of *dividing* and *confiding* everything. God heals us by participating so profoundly in our pain that it becomes part of his eternal life. Sick and despairing men and women have continually experienced and discovered this in every age. I think here of Matthias Grünewald's crucified Christ on the Isenheim altar. He is not merely twisted and disfigured by pain. He is also covered over and over with plague spots. 'He bore our sicknesses', this picture is supposed to tell us; and it said just that to thousands of plague-stricken people who were brought into this church. They saw themselves again in the Man of Sorrows, because he had become one of them. And as they gazed at this picture they experienced eternal, indestructible communion with the crucified God, and in this communion, from which even plague did not sever them, many of them found healing.

In the life, suffering and death of Jesus, we perceive the God who has become human; and this is consolation and salvation for every one of us. Everyone, however handicapped he may be, participates through his life in the divine life. The crucified Christ embraces every life and makes it his own. We who judge according to the standards of our own ideals may think that a blind or deaf or lame or mentally sick person has a 'diminished' life – life which is less than the life of other people. But God loves every human life. So in reality there is no such thing as a diminished life, and no such thing as a handicapped life either. Every life is in its own way divine, and must as such be experienced and respected. On the path of the Son of man from his miserable birth to his prayer in Gethsemane, and then to his death on the cross, every one of us has his place and the point where God identifies himself with him, and where he finds himself accepted. That is the one side of what is meant by healing through community with God.

But there is always the experience of the other side as well: 'God became man that man might become God.' This was the bold statement with which the patristic church described the mystery of the healing of men and women in community with Jesus. Here, becoming God is intended to mean: participating in the superabundant life and indescribable joy of God.

God takes our human life upon himself and makes our weaknesses and handicaps his own, so that he may communicate the livingness of his own life, and his joy. God weeps with us so that we may one day laugh with him. Of course this does not break down all the barriers, or abolish the handicaps. There are certainly 'signs and wonders' in every life, probably more than we realize. But 'the sufferings of this present time' are not as yet 'the glory that is to be revealed'. Still, even now, in this life, we can already experience the certainty that participation in the eternal divine life will wipe away the tears from every eye, because there will be no more crying and no more pain (Rev. 21). If it were not for this hope for eternal life, this life too would lose its meaning.

What is a human being? Who is a human being in the fullest sense of the word? We can now answer this question. A human being – every human being – is the image of the living God. In the crucified Christ everyone can find himself again, because the crucified Christ is reflected in each and all of us, however handicapped we may be. The crucified Son of man is the visible image of the invisible God, and in community with him even people who are handicapped are also his image – every human being with his handicaps.

But anyone who is an image of the living God must also be understood as God's beloved. And anyone who is God's image and his beloved is also his glory and splendour in this world. And anyone who is God's image and splendour in this world is good, true and beautiful, for he corresponds to God in whom everything that is good, true and beautiful has its source. It is true that when we judge by our inhuman standards we often see in other people 'no form or comeliness'. And if we judge ourselves by what we would like to be, we often find 'no beauty' that would make desirable in our own eyes either. But according to God's standards, the others, and we ourselves, are good and beautiful.

Luther once put it like this: 'Sinners are fair because they are beloved. They are not beloved because they are fair.' Human love looks for beauty and flees from what is ugly. But God's love makes sinners righteous and ugly people lovely. So because we are from all eternity God's beloved, we can also love ourselves, and find ourselves good and true and even beautiful, and can find pleasure in what we are. Every one of us is a reflection of God in this world.

There are so many handicapped, sick and disfigured people whose faces and whose bearing reflects the beauty of the divine grace. We must only be alive to it and forget the enervating ideal of beauty propagated by the glossy magazines. Then we will perceive the divine radiance. Beauty is the transfiguration of life through love. Anyone who has ever seen this never forgets it.

Is a handicap an endowment too?

The segregation of handicapped people is a sign of the sickness of our society, in which solidarity and humanity are apparently not as yet considered worth learning by people as a whole. This means that our divided society cannot be healed simply by integrating the handicapped as far as possible into the society of people who do not consider that they are handicapped. Today there is a great deal of talk about this integration. But quite apart from the question of how far any such integration is possible, it would be carried out, not according to the norms of the handicapped but according to the criteria of the non-handicapped. The handicapped would not be taken seriously in the dignity of their own lives and their own world. They would once more have to adapt, in order to lend support to the world and standards of the people who consider themselves to be non-handicapped. No, a real healing of our divided society must bring changes on both sides.

People who think that they are not handicapped must discover the world in which handicapped people live – a world totally unknown to them. They must stop measuring a disability against their own way of living, and seeing it as something negative, and must instead recognize the special and unique experience of life which a handicap offers. They will then learn something from the experience of their handicapped fellow human beings which would otherwise remain a closed book to them. But this means that it is not only the handicapped who have to be integrated into the world of the non-handicapped. The reverse is also true. The non-handicapped must be 'integrated' into the world of the handicapped.

Up to now we allegedly 'normal' people have called another person 'handicapped' if he was *unable to do* this or that. But that is the definition we impose on him. What do we know about what he can do instead, which we cannot do? In the world of the person affected, is the negative aspect of a handicap *really* only negative, and therefore meaningless? Could we not for a change try to discover the positive thing behind a handicap? I believe that I have to thank someone who was allegedly mentally handicapped for a new awareness of the language of the trees.

I should therefore like to put forward the provocative – perhaps even scandalous – thesis that *every 'handicap' is also an endowment.* It is an endowment which we only fail to discover because we fix our gaze on what a person lacks, and what he has been deprived of. But if we were to free ourselves for a moment from the values and standards of our own lives, then we ought really to be capable of understanding the real value of another life and its meaning for us. Everyone concerned might then well ask himself: what meaning has the handicapped person for me and my life? He will then speedily discover the special endowment of that handicapped person.

If we look into the Bible again, we find the astonishing fact that among the gifts and energies of the Holy Spirit (the charismata) the apostle Paul does not list merely powers and abilities; he also talks about sufferings, setbacks and sorrows (II Cor. 4.7ff.). And when he comes to talk about the people whom God has chosen and called for his kingdom, he names first of all weak, despised, foolish and unimportant people. It is with these people that God builds his kingdom, as a judgment on those who believe themselves to be strong, noble and wise (I Cor. 1.26ff.).

The gifts of the Holy Spirit also emerge through the particular situation in which a person is living when God calls him: 'Let every one lead the life which the Lord has assigned to him, and in which God has called him' (I. Cor. 7.17). This means that being a Jew is an endowment of the Spirit, and so is being a Gentile. To be married and to be unmarried are gifts of the Spirit arising from the call to the community of Christ. Consequently to be handicapped, in whatever way, is also a gift of the Holy Spirit if, in this handicap and with it, a person is called to be God's image and his splendour on earth.

The image Paul uses about the body of Christ also leads us to this positive judgment. The church is the body of Christ. This body consists of many different parts – head and foot, mouth and ear, and so on. There are many members, and these all work together; but it is still a single body. Paul does not expect this body of Christ to be bursting with health. There are weak members, and members that are poorly equipped. And it is to the ill-equipped member that God gives most 'glory' and splendour (I Cor. 12.24), for it is the weak and feeble members which he can best use for his kingdom. Why? Surely because the church is the body, not merely of the risen Christ, but of the crucified Christ too. The astonishing energies of the Holy Spirit manifest God's power of resurrection. But the pains, set-backs, handicaps and sufferings of the Holy Spirit reveal the power of God's suffering. The body of Christ is always at the same time the body of the weak, defenceless and crucified Son of man. And the powers of the risen Christ always exist only in the fellowship of the sufferings of Christ crucified. The circumstances which we call 'handicaps' are gifts of the Holy Spirit, for they can become *a reflection* of the suffering Christ.

The handicapped therefore have a service of love to perform for the rest of our society. We must discover this before we talk about charitable service *on behalf of* the handicapped. Society is always only as strong as its weakest links. So to respect and strengthen these weak links means to strengthen the whole society.

Every handicap in the human sense is therefore in God's sense also an endowment. The handicapped person gives to others a priceless insight into the vulnerability and weakness of human life. Through the handicapped, other people can come to know the real, the suffering, the living God who loves them too with an infinite love.

Healing community

We cannot remove disabilities, but we can overcome the handicapping of the handicapped, and we can heal the sick relationship between people with disabilities and people without them. This is not achieved simply through solicitous care and help. It comes pre-eminently through solidarity and a common life, one with another. Being able to help, and being able to allow oneself to be helped, then emerge from this common life of their own accord.

Friendship is the basis of all mutual help, for friendship combines affection with respect. It is only on this basis of mutual recognition and esteem that the necessary care does not appear patronizing, and help that is enlisted is no longer humiliating.

Wherever handicapped and non-handicapped people learn to live together, the old distinction between people who need help and people who give it, collapses. Both groups learn a mutual give and take, each with his own gifts and each with his own limitations.

Community can heal our divided society – both sides of it. Handicapped and handicapper only experience a new humanity in their community with one another. So we should exert all our energies to build up these communities of handicapped and non-handicapped people.

This is one of the tasks of a Christian congregation. Congregations without handicapped people are handicapped congregations, says a declaration by the World Council of Churches. The fault is not merely a lack of willingness for service in the congregation. The deficiency is due to the fact that we have not yet discovered the Christian community as a community of mutual service, because we have not yet experienced it as a charismatic community. But the gifts of the Holy Spirit are all to be found there. They are merely dormant. If they are roused, every congregation discovers a superabundant wealth of initiatives, powers, money and time to be put at the service of the common life of handicapped and non-handicapped people. It is often only the kindling spark that is lacking.

It is true that local congregations of this kind cannot make homes and institutions for the severely handicapped superfluous. But many handicapped people have only been pushed into homes because 'they are a nuisance'. These people can be taken out of the institutions again and given a home. Charitable care in homes and institutions is never anything but an emergency measure. It ought only to be drawn upon when the ministering community is no longer in a position to look after its handicapped members.

Even this great charitable organization to which I am speaking must not divest the congregations of their own tasks of ministry, and their own powers. This organization grew up, and exists, to teach the congregations the service required of them; for congregations can do something that no large-scale organization can: they can build community and fellowship at the very points where people are actually living and suffering. The special charitable functions which have to be carried out in homes and institutions only work properly on the foundation of 'the universal diaconate of all believers'. I am therefore not at all in favour of turning this work over to the state – or to the church, as a large-scale organization. I see the future for this kind of service in *ministering congregations*.

Let me show what I mean from the other side, too. I am speaking as a member of a congregation. Our congregations have become rigid and poverty-stricken because they have delegated too many functions to specialists. We call a minster for the proclamation of the gospel, appoint a professor for theology, a youth-worker for youth work and a deaconess for the sick. Then we think we have done all that is necessary, and simply sit back and watch to see how well they do their work. As an 'ordinary' member of the congregation, one then feels relieved of a burden, and perceives too late that one is the poorer for it. Members of congregations trust themselves neither to witness to the gospel nor to deal with young people; they consider themselves capable neither of theological thinking, nor of community with the handicapped. 'The church should see to it', we say, and simply pay the dues and donations required of us.

A living congregation only comes into being when we members take back the tasks we have delegated to other people, begin to try out our own capabilities, and get to know what we can really do. What the citizen action groups are for political life, Christian action groups ought to be in the sphere of the church: initiatives in building a common life shared by handicapped and non-handicapped people alike; help in equipping handicapped children for life; self-help organizations for adults; the building of day-centres, etc. I don't need to go into all that here. The general assemblies of the German Protestant church (the *Kirchentage*) have what is called a 'possibilities market'. We ought to take up this idea and discover in every congregation the market of its latent possibilities.

The service of love is in fact inseparable from community. For community comes into being where, in the name of Jesus, people, with all their different aptitudes and weaknesses, begin to live with one another and to be available for one another. And the ministry of love comes into being where, in the name of Jesus, people serve one another, help one another to individual life and liberty, and live together in so doing. Charitable help and fellowship are therefore only two sides of one and the same thing: the healing community.

Healing community is what is needed by the handicapped, so that they may be freed from their isolation and find recognition, with their own lives. Healing community is what is needed by the non-handicapped, so that they may be freed from their narrow-minded self-seeking and their fear of life, and find recognition, with their own lives. Healing community is what is needed by our world, where everything is a matter of administration. It is needed so that more humanity and kindness may spread, and so that we may all learn again to love the life which we have received together and for one another, out of the love of God.

18 The Ministry of the Whole Church to the World

I have some difficulty with the subject you have given me for this lecture. The reason is very simple: the theme is too big for me, and I am not up to the theme. I am incapable of surveying 'the whole church'; nor do I really know which 'world' is meant. Is it the so-called First World – the world of Western industrialized society – or 'the Third World'? The world of the present or the world of the future? I certainly have no wish to set myself up as if I were able to treat the subject in its whole breadth and scope; so I have decided to reduce it to the modest dimensions I feel capable of dealing with. I shall not attempt the impossibility of trying to survey 'the whole church' and 'the whole world', like some angel from heaven. Instead, I should like to look up to the mountains of the problem from my own worm's eye view, trying to say what I can see for myself. So what is my standpoint and my own perspective on the questions we have to consider here?

When I talk about this subject I am talking as someone living in the industrial West; as a member of what is known as bourgeois society; as a male member of that society; as a professor of theology who was once a pastor and is now a layman; and finally as a Christian living in Germany, a member of a Protestant established church. I may have other characteristics as well, but these will be enough to show that in some way I combine the three elements of our subject: the ministry, the church, and the world. In my own personal life these three words, ministry, church and world, mean tension, conflict and hope: I have to find out how I can be a pastor and a layman at the same time; how I can live as both a professional theologian and an ordinary Christian; and I also have to discover how I can live with any decency at all as a member of 'the First World' in the face of the Third.

All I can do in considering this huge theme is to try to tell you what is being talked about at the moment in the churches in Germany, small and limited though these are – what is being discussed there about *what it means to be a Christian in any authentic sense* and *what form the church should take* in society if it is to be convincing. I am going to take the phrase 'the whole church' to mean, not the church in the whole world, but the community of clergy and laity in the wholeness of a Christian community. I am going to understand 'the world' as meaning the industrial West, the European world or – to narrow it down further still – West German society as it actually is. You will then easily be able to discover for yourselves the analogies and differences compared with 'the whole church' (Anglican or Catholic or Methodist) in 'the secular world' of Great Britain.

To whom does the church minister in society?

Before anyone says a single word in church, the church itself has already spoken. It has spoken through the form it takes in society. Before we do anything at all in church, the church has already acted. It has acted through its tradition. The church's social and political form and its cultural tradition are a continual witness. The only question is: a witness to what and a witness to whom? To the Lord to whom the church appeals, when it calls itself the church of Jesus Christ? Or to the society, with all its powers and potentialities, in which the church exists? Or does it always witness to both of these simultaneously?

The church always belongs *within the context of the world*, whether it likes it or not. Even if the clergy and the laity are concerned only with themselves and their own internal problems in the church, the world still has its word to say. If some people fail to notice this, it is only because they represent the world's interests themselves, in pious guise. The church is sure to be most misused politically at the very moment when it wants to be totally 'non-political'. This means that it is quite essential for the church, every minister and every congregation, to see themselves as far as possible *in context*, and to become involved, with all their minds and capacities, in the conditions, powers and potentialities of the society they are living in. But the context is not the text, and we must never allow it to become so. The church's *context* is society. But its *text* is *the gospel of Jesus Christ* as this is witnessed to in Holy Scripture. Were it not for the Bible and the preaching of the gospel of Christ according to biblical testimony, the church would long since have been absorbed into the social context, and would be nothing more than the 'civil religion' of society, which is to say a religious reflection of its environment and 'public opinion'. Were not it for the continual realized presence of the crucified Christ in the eucharist through the Spirit of the resurrection, the church would be no more than a public religious institution: it would do nothing but reflect the religious needs and interests of society. But if the gospel of Christ is preached publicly and unremittingly, and if the crucified Christ is made present to the gathered people through bread and wine, then what the church will reflect, and what it will testify to – in its public form as well – is Christ and his liberating and redeeming lordship.

But this means that there will be tensions between text and context. This is the permanent tension between the rule of Christ, which the church proclaims and within which it tries to live, and the powers and potentialities of the society in which, with which, and under which the church exists. This conflict cannot be resolved, either in the one direction or in the other. Every generation has to endure this conflict and carry it through productively. The realized presence of the crucified Christ means that the church can never be quite at home in any society, not even in the best of all possible societies. It will always be something of 'a stranger and a sojourner', until the appearance of the kingdom of God. And this alien and alienating quality is an inescapable part of the witness to Christ. It is not the 'unworldliness' or 'otherworldliness' which people make kindly jokes about, when they come across it in certain clergy and professors. It is the cross of Christ and the preparedness for radical discipleship which – as the Epistle to Diognetus puts it – makes 'every home a foreign land and every foreign land a home' for Christians. For Christ's sake, Christians become 'strangers in their own country', if they have to live under dictatorships, for example, or in racist, class or male-dominated societies.

The church exists in the conflict between the lordship of Christ and the powers and forces of society. In this conflict it has to find its own authentic and convincing form; and this means its testimony to Christ in a world where it will face attack, contradiction, or indifference. That is the reason why the church has laid on it the task of permanent reformation: *ecclesia reformata* and *semper reformanda*. There is no other way of living with Christ's text in this world's context.

So what is the church in our world today? Is it a religious copy *of* society? Or is it Christ's witness *for* society? Is it a factor which helps to stabilize conditions of rule in the First World? Or is it an element of liberation in the Third? Is it something that separates people from one another? Or something that builds community?

Established church – free church – 'bourgeois' church – dialogue church

The Protestant established churches in Germany are together called a *Volkskirche* – a church for the whole people. In word and spirit they certainly stem from the Reformation. But their public form goes back to the turning-point under Constantine, when the church became for the first time an imperial and state church. This turn of events brought an inner contradiction with it. The emperor Constantine made a 'permitted religion' out of persecuted Christianity. His successors Theodosius and Justinian elevated Christianity into the 'official religion' of the state. This threw open the whole Roman empire to the mission and dissemination of the Christian faith. But for this the church had to pay a high price: it had to take over the role of the political religion that was needed so that all the different nations could be integrated into the Roman empire. Now the church was there for everyone. Its mission reached everyone. But as what? It reached everyone only as a component part of the political order – as the state religion of the imperial government.

The result was that the church lost the visible form of community. Because (since all were Christians) the community of the church and the civic community now coincided, the church was organized into parishes, dioceses, territorial and national churches, according to the political districts, regions and territories. The priestly office took on an authoritarian character: the preacher became the lord and master of his parish. The division between clergy and laity became complete. People no longer became members of the church of their own free will, because they believed. They were now members of the church because they were born into it. Community *in* the church was replaced by community *with* the church. In this way what we nowadays call 'the church from above' came into being, the church which takes care of the people, but in which the people themselves have no say. This is the church as hierarchy, as 'holy rule', but not the gathered congregation, the assembled people of God.

You might well think that this form of the church in middle-class or 'bourgeois' society would have been superseded since it is no longer capable of conveying the testimony to Christ. But in Germany this is far from the case. On the contrary: this established church is showing itself to be fairly stable. Over ninety per cent of the population belongs to it, in either its Roman Catholic or its Protestant form. But only a few people participate in it actively – about ten per cent of all Protestants and twenty-five per cent of Catholics. There is a wide cleft between membership of the church and participation in it. Paradoxically, the passivity of its members is the very basis on which the established church operates. If all Christians were active members, this church *for* the people would cease to exist, and a new church *of* the people would come into being. But this is not at all what the organizers and theologians of the established church want.

What they would like to do would to make this old established church into a modern institution for the religious care of the whole people. Through team parishes, centres for pastoral care and counselling, charitable organizations, and the presence of specialized clergy in all spheres of life, from government to the prisons, a network of spiritual security is spread out over the whole of society. Organized religion relieves men and women of the question about the meaning of life. It frees them from having to make their own decisions in questions of faith and morals. It accompanies them at life's key moments with helpful rituals and symbols. Its priests and pastors come to confer significance, to be there at times of crisis, and to help generally in the lives of the people as a whole. This modernization of the old state church, which turns it into the organized religion of industrial society, certainly also throws the church open for everyone. But it is only by chance and incidentally that it has anything to do with Christ. It is losing its Christian identity. The more open and general the offer of organized religion is, the less commitment it demands.

The product of organized religion is an *institutionalized absence of commitment*. Faith becomes a private affair, and the articles of the creed can be replaced at will. This, then, is a religion that demands nothing; so it ceases to console anyone either. Of course one can talk about God, but one no longer worships him. This is the 'gentle Jesus meek and mild', without the cross. This is the justification of what exists, but without judgment.

What this bourgeois religion offers is what Dietrich Bonhoeffer called 'cheap grace'. My Roman Catholic friend Baptist Metz has called it 'the service church', which aims to offer everyone whatever they want. You can help yourself, as you do in a supermarket. This is not merely a critical judgment; it is unfortunately a sad reality, especially in the 'electronic church' that we find in the United States, which, by the cheap sale of religious commodities, and by collecting a great deal of money, is destroying communities and congregations belonging to all the Christian churches. Today this electronic church is also the instrument of the political religion of conservative power politics in America. This became evident at President Reagan's election.

Apart from this development from state church to service church, we find two other forms of the church in middle-class religion. One of them is the free church congregation. The other is the open dialogue church.

The free church congregation is a voluntary community. Consequently people find there what they miss in the established church: personal decision; fellowship with like-minded people; the community which everyone makes his own concern; and an alternative to the anonymous society they otherwise live in. On the continent of Europe it was the Code Napoleon which provided the official basis for the rise of the free churches, by ensuring the right of free association. In the United States, the public system of voluntary religion grew up together with the American republic. Here the church exists solely in its congregations, and the congregations are what their members make them, from their forms of worship to their finances. The separation between church and state made way for this general congregationalism. Democratic respect for the freedom of the individual promoted the voluntary nature of the congregations. In the free church congregations there are no superiors and no subordinates. The pastor is a brother among brothers and sisters. There is no longer 'holy rule', though there is perhaps 'the holy society'.

This brings me to some points of criticism. What the visitor from the Old World notices about the New is the motley variety of denominations in every street. So no one has to put up with conflicts in his own congregation. Everyone can change over to the congregation that happens to suit him. And in the competition on the religious market, the winner – as in other markets too – will be whoever has the cheapest and most entertaining offer. Finally, the church as a free association, or a kind of club, easily falls victim to the seduction of 'class' churches, in which social 'like' is drawn to 'like': birds of a feather flock together. The person who is out for social advancement readily adopts the denomination of the class above his own.

Excellent though the demand for the personal decision of faith and the experience of the voluntary congregations are, the free churches too are not free of the desolation of bourgeois religion: the pluralism of what is offered, the private and arbitrary nature of the decision and, going together with that, the personal, unmoved detachment of their middle-class members.

The open dialogue church seems to be best able to meet the interests of educated men and women in our society. The person who has learnt to think and decide for himself is no longer in need of the church which looks after people, or its spiritual leaders. He does not conform to what the church commands in matters of sexual morality; what it says is often so much a matter of indifference to him that he does not even bother to contradict it. The church's dogmas make no impact whatsoever on his sceptical mind. The voluntary associations of the free churches are too petty-bourgeois for him. He does not like to bind himself to anything. So the educated person, the intellectual, preserves a critical detachment towards all the forms of the church we have discussed. He may at most go to church at Christmas time, for his children's sake. All the same, he does not actually leave the church – at least not in Germany. For he is quite interested in Christianity. So theological books for the general reader have a wide circulation with us. What the intellectual is really looking for is a church that is capable of dialogue and prepared for dialogue. He does not like listening to sermons, but he enjoys talking to intelligent clergy. In Germany, this is the class that provides the hundreds of thousands who attend the General Assemblies (*Kirchentage*) of the Protestant or Catholic churches every two years, even though they never enter a church at any other time. The Protestant and Catholic academies which were founded after the war meet this interest. In this type of Christianity, faith is a permanent question, and disbelief takes the form of a permanent discussion with the church. Here the church is no longer able to take its stand as the possessor of the truth.

It has to expose its dogmas and its ethics to public discussion. It has to learn tolerance. If one is a partner, and no longer a superior, one has to recognize that something true may occur to the other person too. Some churches, and a good many church leaders, find this difficult.

Yet even this church as dialogue is still all too often confined within the constricting bounds of middle-class religion. Discussion about faith then becomes a substitute for faith itself, and all conversations lack binding force. This leads to 'religion without decision', to 'the church without community' and to the irrelevance of the gospel.

Before we now look round for alternatives for a convincing and authentic church, let us sum up this criticism in the light of our subject, 'the ministry of the whole church to the world'.

(*a*) In the establishment '*church from above*', the professional activity of the clergy on the one hand corresponds to the passivity of the well-looked-after laity on the other. There can be no question of a 'ministry of the whole church'. The modernized form of this pastoral church is no different. Here, too, there is a gulf between the pastors and the people they take care of. The priest or minister is there for everyone, but who is actually there for him? Does the minister really feel himself to be a member of his congregation? Is he its pastor as a member of it? Or is he only a member of his congregation as its pastor? In the electronic church, finally, the management remains invisible altogether. Religion is only played-at, on the television screen: it is a pretence of religion.

(*b*) It was *the free churches* which made the first attempt to activate 'the whole church' to ministry for the world. The preacher is recognized as 'brother' by the congregation. Yet, particularly in the smaller groups, the tone is often highly authoritarian. The voluntary act of joining the church does not guarantee freedom in the church itself, any more than it guarantees faithfulness to that church. Consequently the preacher has often enough to be the stimulator and entertainer of his congregation, in order to keep it alive.

(*c*) *The dialogue church* is certainly able to create a sphere free of any kind of domination, in which public discussion about religion and faith can be fearlessly carried on. If the church throws itself open to discussion, then there are merely different discussion partners. The discussion is carried on not only by theologians, but by lay Christians as well. But in this liberal atmosphere of dialogue, 'ministry' in the real sense stops; for the very premise of the discussion is equality.

The whole church and its ministry to the world

With us, attempts to get beyond the individualism and the uncommited nature of middle-class religion are still at the experimental stage. We can learn most from the 'basic communities' and the new Christian communities (Taizé or Iona). But what can we learn from them, and what can we carry over into our own churches?

(a) First, the community of Christians becomes the subject of its own history. We can talk about 'a ministry of the whole church' only when the church becomes a subject of its own, a subject capable of action. State churches, established churches for the people or service churches are none of them the subjects of their own history, with their own capacity for action. In the church's districts and parishes, an individual history is hardly ever experienced or registered, because what the churches cling to and celebrate is merely the eternal cycle of the church's year. How do churches become independent? We know the answer to this from the experiences of the churches which are living in resistance and under persecution.

For one thing, *the one-sided sermon* is supplemented or replaced by the common reading and discussion of the gospel. In this way the gospel enters into the personal history of individuals, and personal life becomes bound to the gospel. An excellent example can be found in Ernesto Cardenal's *The Gospel in Solentiname*, which came out in 1975.

At the same time *the eucharist* becomes the focal point of the congregation, providing the vital power for its fellowship. In the bread and the wine, the presence of Christ is experienced in material, sensory terms, and there the fellowship of his people is physically experienced too. The communion is irreplaceable. There is no substitute for it. The eucharistic community can resist even the electronic church.

It is round the table of their crucified Lord that the beset congregation gathers in all persecuted churches. If the eucharist is linked with a common meal, a worshipping community becomes at the same time a community with a shared, a common life.

Finally, a church like this becomes *a confessing church*. Like the

Reformation church and the Confessing church under the Third Reich, it acknowledges Christ as its only Lord. And that means confessing him as the lord of *its whole life* – not merely personal life, but public life as well; not simply religious life, but political life too. And in this way it declares that it is prepared for resistance against everything that contradicts Christ's promise and his claim.

Churches like this come to realize that they have *a history of their own* with God. They remember special events in their own history. They react to events in public history. In telling their own history they also proclaim the gospel. They have become a subject in God's history, whereas if one reads the annual reports drawn up by pastors in our established church, one cannot even recognize the decade they belong to, because they are so totally detached from any particular period of time.

(*b*) *The second thing we can learn is that the church becomes a liberating community.* A congregation that has become the subject of its own history also takes its own *experience* of community seriously. And by the experience of community I mean the experience of its visible, physical, social form. For the witness of the church, this experience is just as important as word and sacrament. In the church from above it plays no part. But for the church from below, the fellowship its people experience is of fundamental importance. When anyone comes in from outside, the first thing he does is to look at the people who are sitting in church. He does this before he listens to a sermon. But what does he see? A collection of similar, and similarly indifferent, people? Or an assembly of men *and women*, healthy *and handicapped*, working people *and unemployed*, white *and black*, Germans *and immigrant workers*? If the church is not merely the place where we *hear* the gospel, but also the place where we experience it, then the community of Christ must become a healing and a liberating fellowship. Then, through this community, men and women will be healed of the sufferings inflicted on them by a torn and divided society. Then through it, oppressed men and women will be recognized in their dignity and given equal rights. Then lonely people and people who have lost their bearings will find a home there. It delighted and yet shamed me to get a letter recently from a severely handicapped person in which he wrote: 'I have never, all my life, been made so welcome in any community as I have in the church.'

And yet – how many handicapped people are pastors in our church? Women too – second-class citizens in so many civilizations – had this joyful experience of freedom in the early church. In Islamic countries the church makes its impact especially through the dignity of the Christian woman. And yet – how many women are ministers or bishops in our church? Finally, with rising unemployment in the older industrial countries, many people are losing, not only their jobs, but their self-respect as well. By being open for these people, and by initiating ways of self-help, the church can be a liberating community for men and women who are unemployed. What we have known in Germany up to now is 'the church without fellowship', and a multiplicity of groups of similar people in the church. What is laid on us, and what is ahead of us, is the experience of a liberating and healing community at the breaking points of our divided society.

(c) *Lastly, the church becomes the prophetic community.* Let me, in closing, cast a glance at the world-wide church; for overcoming the limitations of bourgeois religion also means overcoming European provincialism. It involves the attempt to make the blind in the First World see. Ecumenically open churches are in the best position for this. They are often the only institutions in our countries which make the problems of the Third World penetrate the awareness of our peoples. Once we perceive that we are members of a world-wide church, the horizon of our lives no longer closes in at the frontiers of our own country or the European Common Market. Today the vast majority of our Christian brothers and sisters are to be found in the Third World. The ecumenical community brings these people before us. As the Third World moves over the horizon of our awareness, we recognize more and more clearly that what are so often called the under-developed nations have become the political and economic victims of European expansion. And we see too *how* this has happened. It also becomes more and more clear to us that our nations are living at the cost of the peoples of the Third World. And we see too *how* this is so. In the slums of the mass cities of the Third World, surely something like the tragedy of the western Gulag Archepelago is being played out. When we begin to look these facts in the face, all that is left to us is either personal and public conversion, and the search for ways to a juster world-wide community, or to close our eyes again as quickly as possible, and to look the other way. The liberation of the oppressed world depends on our conversion; and world peace depends on the liberation of the Third World. When shall we be able to look frankly into the faces of the victims of hunger, exploitation, oppression and persecution in the Third World without being ashamed? In our churches there are many groups who have become sensitive to the presence of the Third World. They are engaged in breaking through the general blindness of our country. But the resistence of bourgeois selfishness is strong. It is only slowly that *a new subject, united in its solidarity*, is crystallizing. And together with this, a new personal sense of solidarity is slowly growing up too. The individualism of middle-class religion and its lack of commitment can be overcome if we find ourselves and the meaning of our lives in the community which confesses Christ, liberates the men and women who have been debased and humiliated, and makes itself one with people all over the world.